# A Lot to Learn

**Canadian Cataloguing in Publication Data**

Main entry under title:

A lot to learn: education and training in Canada

Issued also in French under title: Les chemins de la compétence.
Includes bibliographical references.
ISBN 0-660-14436-0
DSS cat. no. EC22-182/1992E

1. Education, Secondary – Canada – Evaluation.
2. Career education – Canada – Evaluation.
3. Professional education – Canada – Evaluation.
I. Economic Council of Canada. II. Title: Education and training in Canada.

LC1035.8.C2L67 1992     373'.0971     C92-099673-6

# A Lot to Learn

**Education and Training in Canada**

A Statement by the
Economic Council of Canada
1992

© Minister of Supply and Services Canada 1992

Available in Canada through

Associated Bookstores
and other booksellers

or by mail from

Canada Communication Group – Publishing
Ottawa, Canada K1A 0S9

Catalogue No. EC22-182/1992E
ISBN 0-660-14436-0

Printed in Canada

# Contents

| | |
|---|---|
| **Foreword** | vii |
| **Introduction** | 1 |
| **Quality: An Essential Issue** | 4 |
|   Indicators of Quantity | 4 |
|     Enrolment and Drop-out Rates | 4 |
|     The Situation of the Aboriginal People | 6 |
|   Indicators of Quality | 6 |
|     Academic Achievement | 7 |
|     Functional Literacy of Young Adults | 8 |
|   Some Crucial Aspects of Educational Achievement | 9 |
|     Students | 9 |
|     Families, Friends, and Peers | 10 |
|     Teachers | 11 |
|     Schools and School Resources | 12 |
|     The Opportunity to Learn | 13 |
|   Summary | 15 |
| **The Learning Continuum** | 16 |
|   Vocational Education in Secondary Schools | 17 |
|   Colleges | 18 |
|   Apprenticeship | 20 |
|     National Standards and Costs | 20 |
|     Responsiveness of the Apprenticeship System | 21 |
|   Continuous Skill Upgrading | 22 |
|     Skill Needs and Employers' Responses | 22 |
|     Employer-Based Training | 23 |
|     A Role for "Distance" Education | 24 |
|   The Need for Change | 24 |
|     Enhancing Coherence | 24 |
|     Promoting Partnerships | 25 |
|     Developing Cooperative Programs | 25 |
| **The Teaching Profession** | 26 |
|   A Profile of Teachers in Canada | 26 |
|   Teacher Demand and Supply | 27 |
|   Teacher Training | 28 |
|   Teachers' Earnings | 28 |
|   Career Structure | 30 |
|   Summary | 31 |

| | |
|---|---|
| **Costs and Financing** | **31** |
|     Financial Commitment to Education | 31 |
|         International Comparisons | 31 |
|         Spending by the Provinces | 33 |
|     The Financing of Education | 38 |
|     Summary | 39 |
| | |
| **Education and Training: An International Perspective** | **39** |
|     Canada's International Standing | 40 |
|         An Uneven Record | 40 |
|         Strengths . . . | 40 |
|         . . . and Weaknesses | 41 |
|     Lessons from Japan and Germany | 42 |
|         Social Cohesion | 42 |
|         Curriculum Options vs. a Standard System | 42 |
|         Committed Employers | 44 |
|         Careers and Continuous Learning | 44 |
|         The Role of Government | 45 |
|     Summary | 46 |
| | |
| **Conclusions** | **47** |
|     Targets | 48 |
|     Indicators | 50 |
|     Directions for Change | 51 |
|         Towards a Comprehensive System | 51 |
|         Towards an Open System | 54 |
|         Towards a Responsive System | 56 |
|         Towards a Relevant System | 56 |
|     Concluding Comments | 58 |
| | |
| **References** | **59** |
| | |
| **List of Tables and Figures** | **61** |
| | |
| **Members of the Economic Council of Canada, as of February 25, 1992** | **63** |
| | |
| **Project Team** | **65** |

# Foreword

*A Lot to Learn* is the first comprehensive examination of the way primary and secondary schools and the training system in Canada prepare young people for employment. Members of the Economic Council identified the need for a study of education and training in the late 1980s and early 1990s as they worked on a number of Council studies – *Making Technology Work, Good Jobs, Bad Jobs*, and most recently *Pulling Together*. In each of these major projects, it became clear that the high levels of participation in education obscured high rates of illiteracy and unemployment, and serious mismatching between jobs and skills.

Our findings confirm that education is a cumulative process – skills that are learned well in the early years provide the foundation for future success. And early setbacks in learning are hard to correct, often leading to dropping out, followed by a lifetime of low wages and unstable employment patterns.

Our research also shows that employers and parents – and indeed, society as a whole – give conflicting signals to students and teachers. This lack of "coherence" is most evident in the transition from school to work. Large numbers of young Canadians do not value education. They cannot see clear pathways from school to work and therefore follow a process of trial and error that is in stark contrast to the clear passages laid out in other industrial countries, particularly Japan and Germany.

We are very much aware that the task facing schools and teachers is much harder than it used to be: social institutions such as the family and the church have been weakened, and the student population has become more diverse. At the same time, the need for a strong education and training system has increased because the level of skills required in the world of work has escalated as a result of the transition to an information society.

It is our hope that these research findings will shed new light on the system's weaknesses and that the targets and policy directions proposed here will help Canadians to make education and training more effective and more responsive to their needs.

I would like to take this opportunity to thank the project director, Keith Newton (Senior Research Director at the Council), the project staff, and the excellent Advisory Committee, which was chaired by Ken Stickland. I also want to thank Council members – the ones who pointed to the need for this study in 1989 and those who, more recently, have helped to shape the conclusions and policy directions set out in this Statement. While the members whose names are listed at the end of the report had a major influence on these conclusions, the decision to abolish the Economic Council of Canada occurred just days before the final version of the report was ready to be sent out for their signature. Thus they did not have an opportunity to sign this report.

Judith Maxwell
Chairman

# A Lot to Learn

*Upon the education of the people of this country the fate of this country depends.*

Benjamin Disraeli,
addressing the British House of Commons in 1874

## Introduction

Education is the very lifeblood of society, sustaining our endeavours and shaping our prospects. Not only do good citizenship and the democratic ideal depend on a well-informed and well-educated citizenry, but the learning process also makes a critical contribution to creativity and intellectual curiosity.

The impact of education extends to the economic domain. Educational attainment has a strong influence on earnings and employment, and since most Canadian adults participate in the labour market, this link is of vital importance to the economy. Indeed, education is a good investment: after taking account of the direct costs of schooling and of forgone earnings, the additional income from completing secondary school yields a rate of return of some 30 per cent for individuals. We know from past Council work [see *Good Jobs, Bad Jobs*] that better-educated people tend to hold jobs that are more secure and more satisfying. That study also showed that unemployment rates are higher for persons with lower levels of education and that the risk of unemployment that they face has been increasing substantially over time.

The contribution of skill development to economic performance has special significance today when, quite simply, the Canadian economy is under threat. In *Pulling Together*, the Council's recent Statement on the links between productivity, innovation, and trade, we examined the reasons for the longer and deeper slowdown in manufacturing productivity in Canada relative to the United States during the period 1973-85. We found that Canadian manufacturing firms responded less effectively to changes in the real exchange rate and to energy price shocks. They were slower to adopt innovations and labour-saving measures. Our Statement concluded that the problem is systemic – that managers, workers, policymakers, and others have not responded to change effectively.

To improve productivity, trade performance, and innovation – to improve the overall competitiveness of a firm, an industry, or an entire economy – one of the critical factors is the enhancement of human skills. Indeed, individually and collectively Canadians face a painful choice: develop skills or accept low wages. But this begs the question: Do our systems of education and training enable Canadians to meet this challenge? Are we well served, and if not, why not?

Before tackling these issues, we note, first, that the education sector is certainly large in terms of inputs. As Figures 1 through 4 show, the education sector accounts for roughly 5 per cent of gross domestic product (national-accounts basis) and employs close to one million people, or 7 per cent of the total work force. Over 5 million Canadians are enrolled in elementary and secondary schools, and well over a million are in various postsecondary institutions (see box).

By and large, formal education in Canada is provided through public funds. But governments at all levels today face an era of acute fiscal restraint. Thus a major policy concern in future decades will be whether society can maintain and enhance both the accessibility and the quality of the education system without making excessive claims on economic resources.

The private sector also has a major role to play. Canadian industry spends close to $1.5 billion on training programs, and countless workers acquire skills on the job by informal methods. But since the proportion of young workers entering the labour force – the new blood with the fresh ideas and latest techniques – is shrinking, employers must seek innovative approaches to develop the skills of the mature work force.

The sheer size of the education and training systems would justify an examination of their effectiveness. Beyond that, however, the quality of the system has become a matter

---

**Canadians at School**

- There are close to 2.3 million children aged from 0 to 5 years in Canada, about 0.5 million of whom are in preschool programs.
- Some 2.3 million children attend elementary school.
- Nearly 2.3 million students attend secondary school; about 10 per cent of senior high-schoolers are enrolled in vocational programs.
- There are about 120,000 apprentices in Canada.
- There are over 0.5 million students in the college system; well over 200,000 of them are in Quebec's CÉGEP system; private career colleges have about 140,000 students.
- Enrolments in universities are approaching the 1-million mark, with over 12 per cent of students in graduate programs.

2  A Lot to Learn

**Figure 1**

**Gross domestic product: distribution by sector, Canada, 1990**

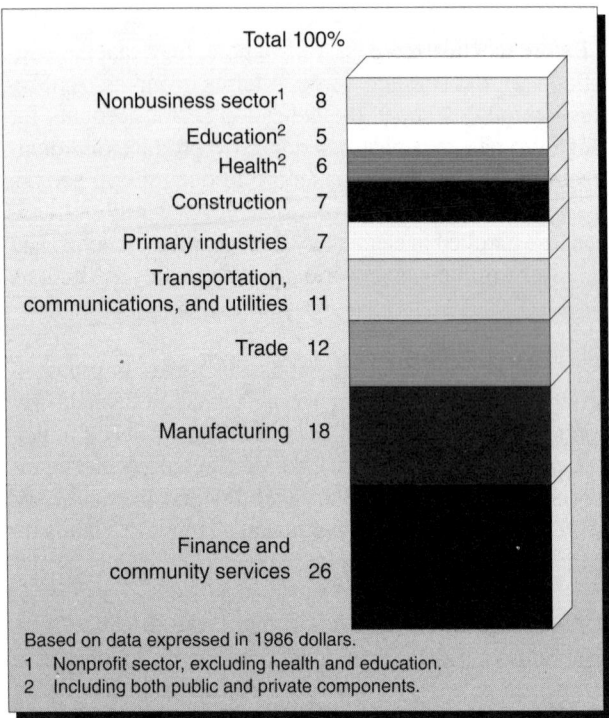

Based on data expressed in 1986 dollars.
1  Nonprofit sector, excluding health and education.
2  Including both public and private components.

**Figure 2**

**Employment: distribution by sector, Canada, 1990**

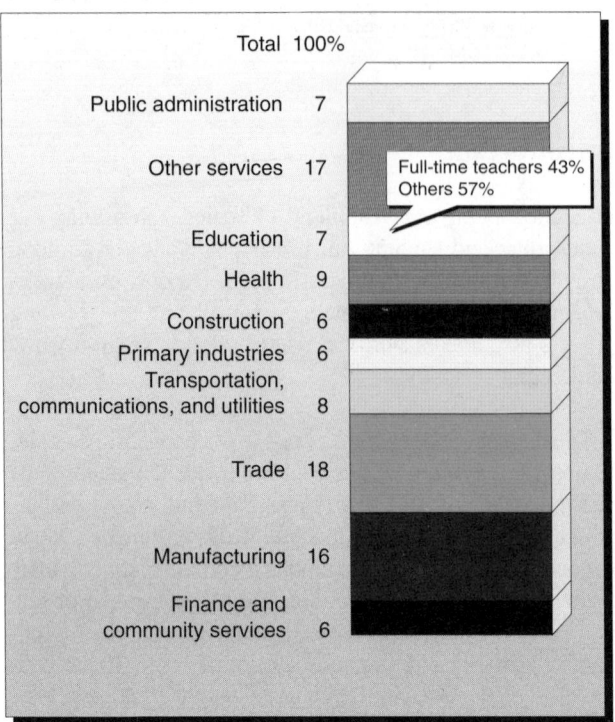

**Figure 3**

**Education expenditures: distribution by level, Canada, 1989-90**

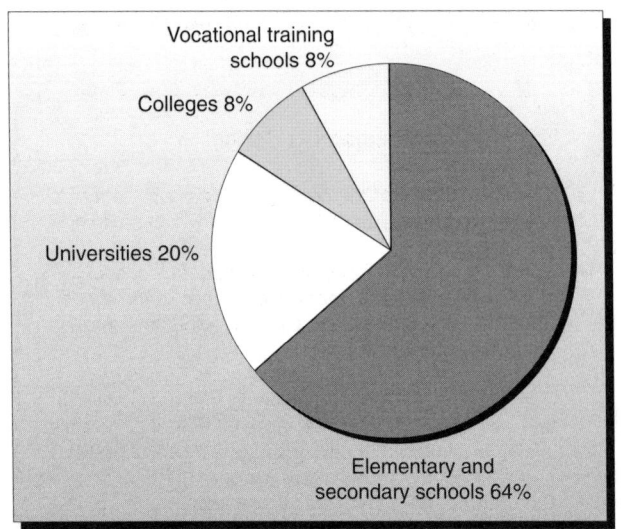

**Figure 4**

**School enrolment: distribution by level of study, Canada, 1989-90**

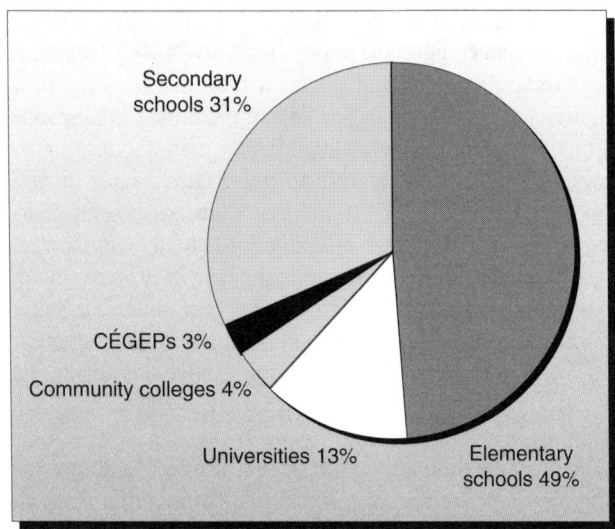

SOURCE   Estimates by the Economic Council, based on data from Statistics Canada.

of serious debate for many citizens. On the one hand, employers are seeking more from the education system. The new jobs that are being created in Canada tend to require a higher level of basic skills in literacy and numeracy, and better problem-solving skills, than the jobs that were being created 10 or 20 years ago. At the same time, we observe high drop-out rates from secondary school, and high rates of illiteracy and innumeracy among young people. And Canada devotes fewer resources to training than do many of its trading rivals.

Until now, however, it has been difficult to say anything definitive about the "output" of the education system. There is a general tendency to measure the system by its inputs, but there has been no systematic effort to evaluate actual performance – the achievement of people leaving the system. At the same time, there is a profound sense of unease about whether the Canadian system is meeting the needs of today's students and, hence, of society at large. Society is changing rapidly in this and other countries. Many developed nations – in particular the members of the Organisation for Economic Co-operation and Development (OECD) – have reformed or are reforming their learning systems to reflect such changes. Canadians, too, need to take a hard look at their own system.

Evaluating the outcomes of that system is no simple task. Nonetheless, the Economic Council has worked to piece together comprehensive documentation on the quality of the elementary, secondary, and training systems across Canada, with a view to establishing a rough set of benchmarks. In many respects, these benchmarks themselves are in need of improvement – there are many areas where we suggest better testing and collection of information. The information that we have gathered, however, does provide Canadians with an objective and substantive assessment of where they stand at the beginning of the 1990s. We also propose directions for reform that, we believe, would lead to better outcomes in the future.

In discussing these issues, we examine, first, various measures of quality, with special emphasis on Canadian students' performance in the acquisition of the "foundation" skills upon which subsequent learning and labour-market experience may be built. Issues such as dropping out and illiteracy are addressed, as well as the level of Canadian students' achievement internationally, interprovincially, and over time.

One conclusion of our research that seems to be accepted universally is that learning is, and must be, continuous. Accordingly, we look at the questions of vocational education and training, and of the linkages between learning and the labour market. That discussion also expands upon the critical role played by "coherence" – defined in Webster's Dictionary as "the quality of being logically integrated, consistent and intelligible." Coherence has two dimensions in the present context: (1) the transmission by employers of signals about skill needs and about the preparation of graduates of the education system; and (2) the accurate reading of those signals by students, parents, and learning institutions – and, most particularly, their response to those signals. A principal conclusion that drives our policy suggestions in the final section is that, at present, the Canadian system lacks coherence and that improvements can be achieved only with a substantially increased involvement – and commitment – of a wide community of stakeholders.

A further aspect of quality is also examined – teachers, the resource most critical to the success of the system. Some of the spending patterns of the system are discussed as well: How much does it cost? How is it funded?

Following this analysis, we attempt to place our findings in a broader perspective. Having assessed various aspects of the Canadian system, how does it measure up on the international scene? We show how the characteristics of the education and training systems, labour-market performance, and overall economic performance are linked. The systems of a number of OECD countries are compared, using this framework. Gaps and deficiencies in the Canadian system are highlighted, and an attempt is made to distil the key ingredients of success – with special emphasis on coherence – from the stellar performers on the international scene.

The final section summarizes our main conclusions. It sets out targets and indicators, advances broad directions for change, and suggests specific policy considerations.

While our focus is primarily economic, we are quite aware that the formal education system, in particular, has a range of valuable objectives that are just as important – some might argue, more important. Still, the vast majority of the young people who pass through Canadian schools are ultimately destined for the labour market. Their future well-being – economic and social – will depend on how well they can exploit their potential in the labour market. Recent work shows that the occupational structure in many countries is becoming polarized into good jobs and bad jobs. Such a trend could eventually threaten the principle of equality of opportunity that underlies the Canadian sense of democracy. Since education and training are one of the principal means by which the polarization trend might be reversed, this Statement can be said to have objectives that far transcend narrow economics.

## Quality: An Essential Issue

We have emphasized the many ways in which education influences society and, in turn, is influenced by it. This diversity is also reflected in the infinite variety of abilities, tastes, temperaments, and ambitions that characterizes the millions of students passing through the Canadian education system each year. Clearly, individuals and society expect many different things from the education system, and no single indicator can summarize our assessment of it. Nor can there be a simple answer to the question of how it can be further improved.

Contemporary society sets very many goals for the education system. A well-known study of American schools [see Goodlad] enumerates 62 goals, arranged in 10 groups under four major headings:

A   Academic goals

    1   Mastery of basic skills and fundamental processes

    2   Intellectual development

B   Vocational goals

    3   Career education – vocational education

C   Social, civic, and cultural goals

    4   Interpersonal understanding

    5   Citizenship participation

    6   Enculturation

    7   Moral and ethical character

D   Personal goals

    8   Emotional and physical well-being

    9   Creativity and aesthetic expression

    10   Self-realization.

A simple, though perhaps too general, definition of the purpose of education is that it prepares young people for the next stage of life. Many of them (and their parents) judge the quality of the education system by its success in preparing students for the labour market. Employment and unemployment statistics show convincingly that there is a clear relationship between years of schooling and labour market success. Furthermore, mastery of basic skills is fundamental to both academic *and* vocational success. Our research indicates clearly that functional literacy "pays" in the sense that it improves one's chance of gaining and retaining employment, of being employed in a better-paying industry and occupation, *and* of earning a higher income in those industries and occupations.

Public opinion polls show that Canadians have diverse expectations about what the education system should accomplish, and contradictory views of how well their schools are functioning. A recent survey reveals that in general, Canadians think their schools have improved. Yet, in judging specific schools, only 45 per cent assign to the school of their community an A or B grade, compared with 59 per cent in 1979. So a declining proportion of people regard their schools as very good, while an increasing number see them as mediocre or worse (55 per cent in 1990, up from 41 per cent in 1979). Public opinion is an unreliable measure of the quality of Canadian education, however. Here, we review the evidence on the achievement of students in Canada and the state of our knowledge about the factors that influence achievement – that is, schools, teachers, family, and other key elements of the system. Our analysis is based on the examination of both quantitative and qualitative indicators of education.

### *Indicators of Quantity*

In education, quantitative indicators measure the accessibility of the system. Canadians' sense of fairness demands that education should be accessible to every young person. This is particularly important at those levels where the economic returns to education are the highest not only for the recipient but also for society as a whole – that is, at the elementary and secondary levels.

### *Enrolment and Drop-out Rates*

With respect to the duration of formal education, Canada compares favourably with other countries. In 1986, the median level of schooling of the population aged 15 and over was 12.2 years. This included well over a million young people who had not yet completed their formal education. For people aged 25 to 44, who had mostly finished formal schooling, the corresponding figure was 12.8 years. These levels are among the highest in the world. And Canada's recent progress is also impressive: in 1971, the median level of schooling of 25-44-year olds was only 11 years.

These successes must not blind us to our shortcomings. Estimates suggest that as many as 30 per cent of our young people do not finish secondary school. This is disturbing, for several reasons. As we shall see later on, Canada's apprenticeship system is weak, and thus drop-outs have only limited opportunity to better themselves when they leave the formal education system. Moreover, dropping out is relatively more frequent among children from poorer families or from broken homes and among those whose parents have lower levels of education and precarious jobs. Thus poverty tends to be a self-perpetuating phenomenon.

The process and nature of dropping out have changed over the past three or four decades. Until 1955, most students who dropped out did so when they reached the age when schooling was no longer compulsory. This has changed in that most students today attempt to continue beyond the legal school-leaving age, but some soon find they do not have the ability or motivation to keep up with their peers in the accumulation of credits needed for a secondary-school diploma. They may miss a credit or two in the first year of senior high school, then another in the next year, and they give up completely in the third. But well before they drop out *de facto*, they have dropped out psychologically. Dropping out is, just like education itself, a cumulative process.

This can be illustrated by the Quebec statistics for 1989-90, shown in Figure 5. Of 100 students enrolled in elementary school, none dropped out before the first secondary grade (i.e., Grade 7). The number of drop-outs rose steadily with each successive grade beyond that level, however, with only 64 students graduating from secondary school (i.e., Grade 11) that year.

It follows that a sudden tightening of requirements for secondary-school graduation will result in a higher drop-out rate. That is indeed what happened in Quebec in 1982-83, when, beginning with the first secondary grade, the pass mark was raised from 50 to 60 per cent. The cumulative drop-out rate rose from about 17 per cent in 1982-83 to about 36 per cent in 1989-90. This strongly suggests that

Figure 5

School and school-leaving probabilities for 100 students entering elementary school, based on findings for 1989-90, Quebec

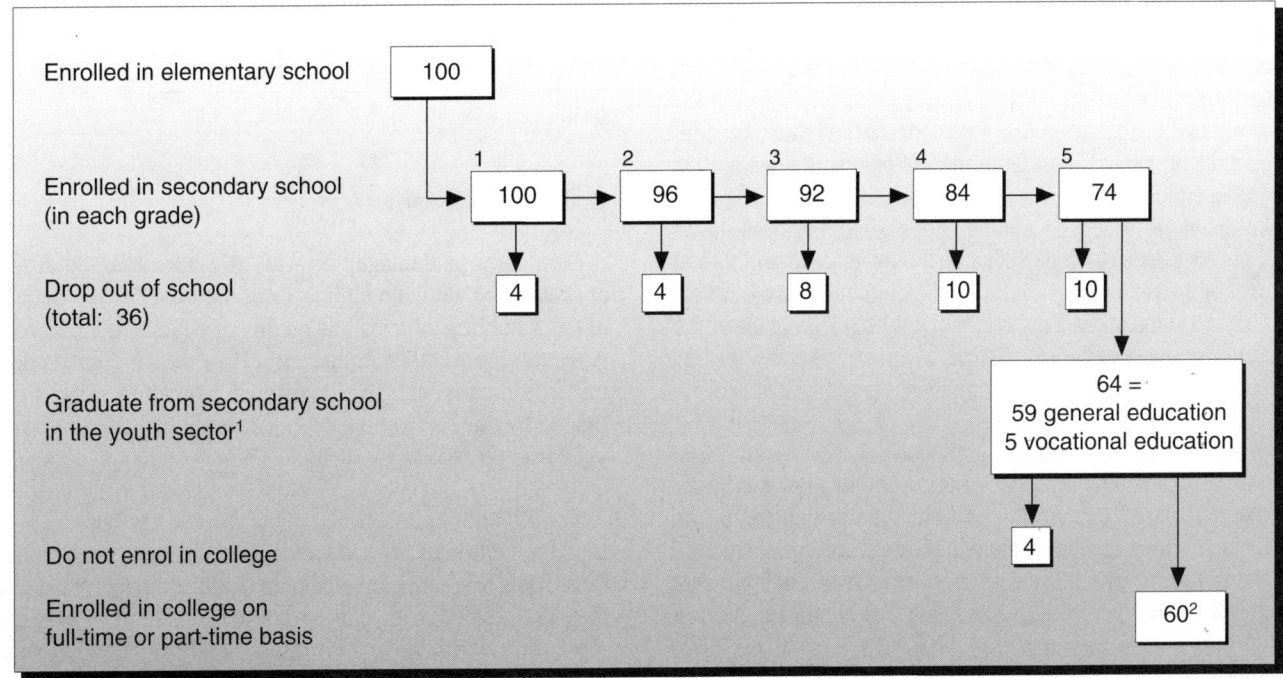

1   Preliminary estimates.
2   Students who enroll in college are not limited to those who graduate from secondary school in the youth sector.
SOURCE   Ministère de l'Éducation, Direction générale de la recherche et du développement, *Education Indicators for the Elementary and Secondary Levels, 1991* (Québec, 1991).

criteria for secondary-school success can be raised only if elementary and secondary education have properly prepared the students for this additional challenge.

The secondary-school drop-out rate is somewhat higher among boys than girls. Ethnic background also has an impact. Children from those cultures which value achievement highly and in which parental influence is strong are less prone to drop out of school. Further analysis would be needed, however, to understand better the links between the high drop-out rates of certain groups and such factors as their socio-economic status, cultural values, the incidence of broken homes, and the tendency for children to ignore their parents' wishes.

*The Situation of the Aboriginal People*

Educational attainment among Canada's Native peoples is weak, compared with that of other Canadians. Native Canadians have been caught in a vicious circle of limited education, unemployment or poorly paid jobs, and poverty. Redressing this situation is an urgent social priority.

While the bulk of the Canadian population is between 25 and 64 years of age, the majority of the Native Indian population is under 25 years. Thus Aboriginal people will make up a growing proportion of new labour-force entrants in the coming years. In fact, in Manitoba and Saskatchewan one in four entrants into the labour force in the 1990s will be Indian. To participate effectively in society – and in the work force, in particular – the population must be adequately prepared. Data from the 1986 census illustrate the gap in educational attainment between the Aboriginal population and the overall Canadian population. Figure 6 shows that, on average, 45 per cent of the on-reserve and 24 per cent of the off-reserve adult Indian population have less than Grade 9 education. This compares with 17 per cent of the non-Indian population. These proportions vary widely across provinces and territories.

Although the education gap between Native and non-Native Canadians is huge, some progress has been made over the past 30 years. For example, the proportion of on-reserve students who remained enrolled continuously until the last grade of secondary school climbed from 3 per cent in 1960 to 44 per cent in 1988; but this is still far short of the national average of about two thirds, which is itself disappointingly low. Another positive sign is the noticeable presence of Native students in postsecondary education (more than 18,500 in 1990). These signs of progress are encouraging, but efforts to close the gap must be redoubled.

**Figure 6**

Proportion of people with less than Grade 9 education among the "registered" Indian population and the general population, Canada, by province or territory, 1986

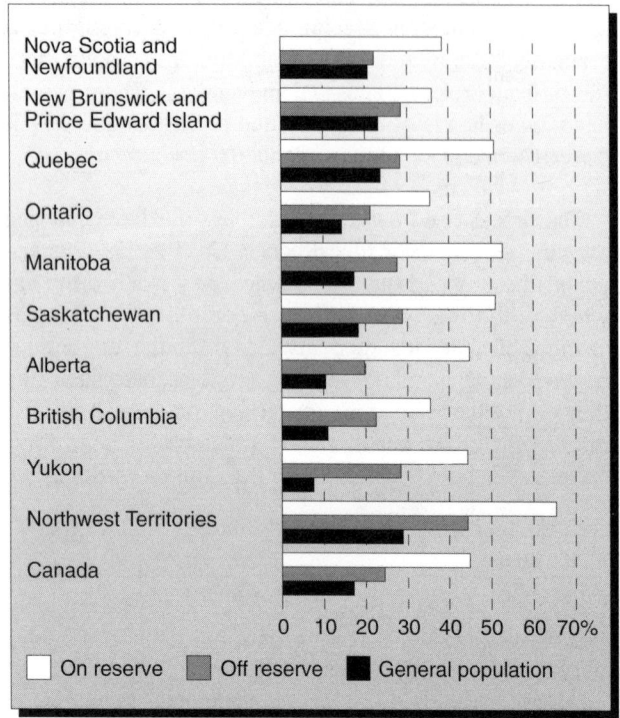

SOURCE   Estimates by the Economic Council, based on data from Indian and Northern Affairs Canada.

*Indicators of Quality*

Enrolment percentages, as well as graduation and drop-out rates, are valuable indicators of the quantitative output of the schooling system. The quality of education, however, is just as important as its quantity. How well is Canada doing in this respect? The quality of education should be judged by measuring how successful schools are at achieving the goals we set for them.

Traditionally, educational achievement has been measured by examinations and tests. These are still the best indicators of academic and vocational achievement, provided they are treated with appropriate caution. This group of indicators deals with the mastery of basic literacy and numeracy skills and with more advanced achievement at school. The basic skills are important, not only by themselves but also because they form the indispensable basis for the achievement of almost all the other goals of education.

And yet, while basic literacy may seem to be a modest aim, Statistics Canada has found that 30 per cent of Canadian adults who have completed their secondary education have difficulty reading and try to avoid situations that require reading. Some 36 per cent of adults in the same group cannot perform simple sequences of numerical operations that would enable them to meet most everyday demands. Given such numbers, what can we expect from those who do *not* complete secondary schooling?

Much less work has been done in the measurement of the achievement of social, civic, cultural, and personal goals through education. Research on effective schools suggests, however, that schools which score high on imparting knowledge (cognitive achievement) tend to do well on these other goals as well.

The focus on the achievement of cognitive goals should not be interpreted as lack of interest in the other goals. It merely acknowledges that high achievement in the cognitive field – particularly the full mastery of basic skills and fundamental processes – is the indispensable precondition for a first-class vocational education and for the attainment of social, cultural, and personal goals. Also, research findings suggest that better-educated persons are more likely to take advantage of "recurrent" education later in life, after the completion of formal youth education. Recurrent education, which is often pursued as a means to attain cultural or personal goals, therefore tends to build upon early achievement. Only seldom can it fully compensate for dropping out or for mediocre performances in youth.

*Academic Achievement*

*International Comparisons* — Our knowledge of academic achievement in Canada is fragmentary and mostly based on international studies. But making fair international comparisons of academic achievement is difficult. The school systems of various countries differ in many respects. Selective systems, such as those of England or Hong Kong, are more likely to retain the most able students, which tends to raise the average achievement of those who complete secondary school, relative to countries like Canada, where the policy is to retain a large percentage of an age cohort until secondary-school graduation. Some countries – Hungary, for example – leave students little freedom in the choice of subjects. Thus the wide compulsory participation in, say, mathematics tends to lower the average achievement. Others, like Canada or England, permit much more choice in the later years of secondary school. In these countries, only those students who are relatively strong in a particular subject will participate in it. Some education systems end secondary school with Grade 11, many with Grade 12, a few with Grade 13 (or some equivalent). The additional years of schooling could be expected to have a positive influence on academic achievement. In our work, we have adjusted the raw findings for these potentially distorting factors.

Our results for science and mathematics can be summarized as follows. At age 10, Canadian children compare favourably with those in most industrialized countries. By age 13 or 14, Canada's relative position deteriorates somewhat, though the evidence on this is mixed. By the end of secondary school, Canada's achievement is weak, when adjusted for years of schooling, retention rates, and freedom of subject choice. This result is particularly pronounced in science, but it seems to hold for mathematics as well. We conclude that Canadian children receive a good start, but from the age of 13 or 14, they begin gradually to fall behind children in other countries.

*Interprovincial Comparisons* — The Second International Science Study [see Crocker] indicates that after adjustment for selectivity and years of schooling, students in the western provinces achieve better results than those in the central provinces, while these, in turn, outperform students in the Atlantic provinces (Figure 7). Similar results are found in Statistics Canada's Survey of Literacy Skills Used in Daily Activities (1989), as well as in the Southam Literacy Survey (1987).

The poorer performance of the eastern provinces can be explained, in part, by lower spending per student and by lower per-capita income, which is an indicator of both fiscal capacity and socio-economic status. However, an important part of the poorer performance of the central and eastern provinces relative to the West cannot be explained by the factors that we tested – that is, gender; age; migrant status; language; years of schooling; type of schooling (academic or vocational); education of parents; rural or urban residence; size of city; health and learning handicaps.

At the same time, even after adjusting for these factors Ontario does less well than one might expect on the basis of spending per student and of per-capita income. This is most evident in Ontario's very weak performance in the mathematics portion of the Second International Assessment of Educational Progress [see Lapointe et al.]. Quebec and Nova Scotia children, on the other hand, showed strong achievement. In our view, these interprovincial differences are cause for deep concern and warrant further research. Raising the performance of the weaker provinces would contribute to an improvement in overall Canadian performance. Further analysis of this question will be found in our more detailed research report on education, to be released later this year.

#### Figure 7
#### Science achievement at the end of secondary school, Canada, by province, mid-1980s[1]

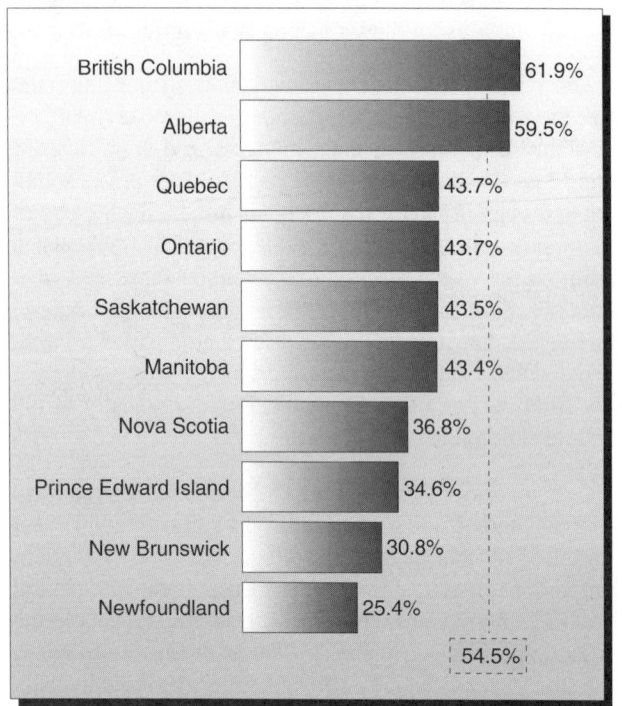

1   The population measured here consists of students in the final year of secondary school with a strong scientific component in their academic program. The SISS results are adjusted for years of schooling and retention rates. The mean for the 15 "countries" (including two Canadian provinces and two grade levels in Hong Kong) taking part in the study was 54.5 per cent. The test was administered over the period 1983-86.
SOURCE   Estimates by the Economic Council, based on the findings of the Second International Science Study [see Crocker] and on data from Statistics Canada.

*Intertemporal Comparisons* — There is very little dependable information on intertemporal comparisons of educational achievement for Canada as a whole. The provincial departments of education do have various achievement-assessment programs of their own, but the results are not comparable across provinces, and sometimes are not comparable over time even within the same province. The only consistent indicator is the Canadian Test of Basic Skills (developed by Nelson Canada, a private firm), which provides comparable achievement data in vocabulary, reading, language skills, work-study skills, mathematics, and a composite score. Unfortunately, the test does not measure achievement in science. Test results are available for a representative sample of English-language schools in Canada (except those in Quebec) for 1966, 1973, 1980 and 1991 (Figure 8).

The composite score indicates a deterioration equivalent to 7.6 per cent between 1966 and 1973 for Grade 8 students.

The steepest decline (11.5 per cent) was in language skills. There was some improvement between 1973 and 1980, but the scores remained below the 1966 level. There was a slight deterioration between 1980 and 1991. Altogether, the loss between 1966 and 1991 is equivalent to 6.3 per cent. The results suggest that average achievement in the tested subjects has not improved, but rather has deteriorated over the past 25 years.

The poorest showing is in the language skills. This is also the area giving rise to the largest number of complaints from employers about prospective labour-market entrants. The deterioration of performance among young people is also confirmed by Statistics Canada's Functional Literacy Survey: the 16-24-year-old group was performing worse than 25-34 and 35-44-year olds. Note also that even as test results deteriorated between 1966 and 1991, the student/teacher ratio declined by about one third, while expenditures per student, adjusted for inflation, more than doubled. Does this mean that the most recent entrants into the student population are more difficult to teach? Or does effective teaching depend on factors other than smaller classes and more generous spending?

*Functional Literacy of Young Adults*

The disturbing findings of Statistics Canada's 1989 Survey of Literacy Skills have been widely publicized. Some 38 per cent of Canadians aged 16 to 69 "do not meet everyday reading demands"; a similar proportion "have not mastered the skills needed to deal with everyday numeracy operations." Of course, older people have received less schooling than the younger-age cohorts, and so their scores will tend to lower the average. In addition, if those who received their education outside Canada display any skill shortcomings, this cannot be held against the Canadian education system. Nevertheless, even the youngest group (aged 16 to 24) of those born in Canada showed appallingly high functional-illiteracy rates, though practically all of them must have received at least nine years of compulsory education. More than 28 per cent of this group were below the everyday reading level, and more than 44 per cent fell short of the numeracy requirements.

If these figures do not improve, our school system will produce well over *one million* new functional illiterates over the next 10 years. This is a most alarming prospect, and our *first priority* must be to prevent it. It is unacceptable that after nine years of schooling and at the age when they are legally able to enter the labour force, so many Canadians cannot meet the very modest requirements of the Statistics Canada survey.

**Figure 8**
**Results of test of basic skills, in Grade 8 students, Canada,[1] 1966, 1973, 1980, and 1991**

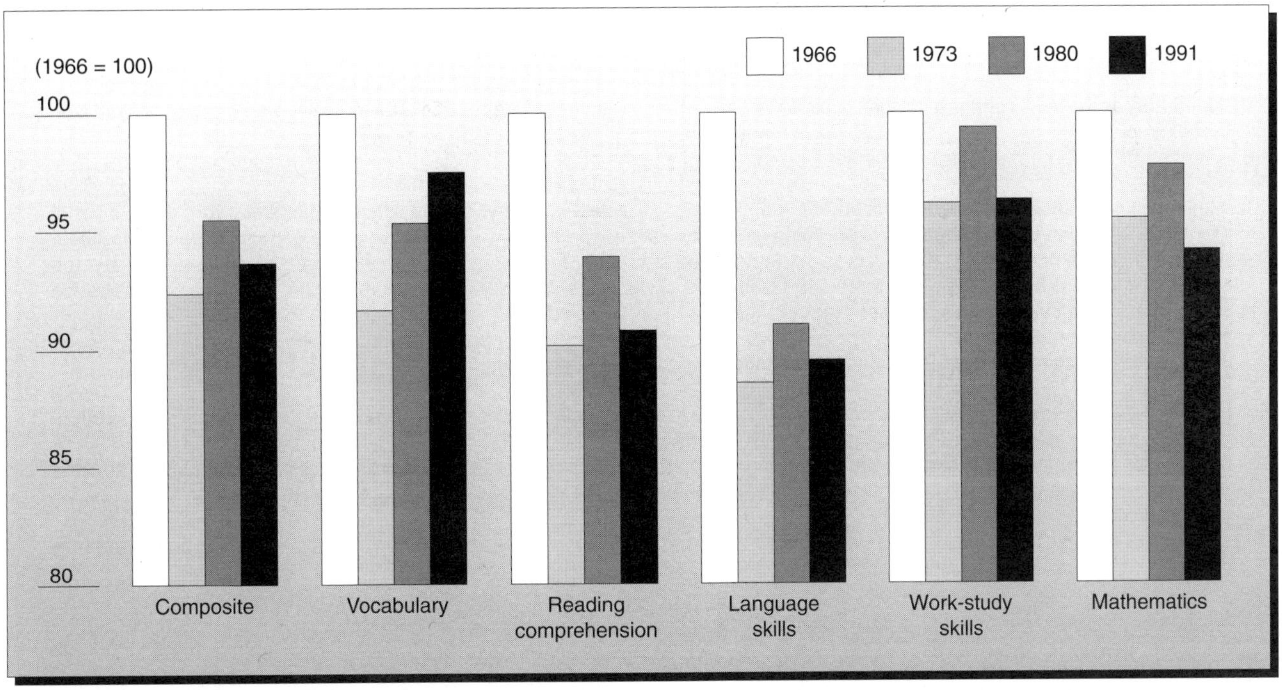

1  English-language schools only, excluding those in Quebec.
SOURCE  Based on data from Nelson Canada.

## Some Crucial Aspects of Educational Achievement

The forces and characteristics that influence educational achievement merit close scrutiny. In examining this issue, we discuss, in turn, the students themselves; their families, friends, and peers; teachers; schools and school resources; and learning opportunities, as reflected in the curriculum.

### Students

Two simple facts must be kept in mind when thinking about educational achievement: 1) *education is a cumulative process*; and 2) *motivation is critical for achievement, and achievement acts as an important motivator.*

These two facts have important consequences. Most children are interested and motivated when they start school, but with the passage of time, those who have not mastered some aspect of a subject tend to fall further and further behind. They would have to make an extra effort to catch up with the rest of the class. As for the teacher, she/he has now to care for the laggards, as well as to ensure the progress of those who have mastered the material. The consequence can be illustrated with data from student-attitude surveys of the Edmonton Public School District. One of the questions was: "Do you feel good about (are you satisfied with) how much you are learning?" In the kindergarten-to-Grade-3 group, 90 per cent answered "yes" over the 1985-90 period. For Grades 4 to 6, the corresponding proportion was 84 per cent; for Grades 7 to 9, 72 per cent. Interestingly, the 28 per cent of this latter group who replied "no," "not sure," or refused to answer, correspond roughly to the proportion of those who tend to drop out before completing secondary school. Continuous monitoring of the students' progress and nourishing a sense of accomplishment are among the most important contributors to educational success. Note that it is the *gain* in achievement, not the *level* of achievement, that gives satisfaction to the student and is the proper indicator of the quality of teaching. The evaluation of progress can take many forms. Testing, if well done, comes closest to an objective quantitative judgment of progress (see box on p. 10).

Doing well in school is a powerful motivator, but it is often not enough. The young do rise to the challenge if they see a reason to exert themselves. Unfortunately, for those who complete secondary school but do not intend to go on to postsecondary education, there is little inducement to

> **Testing**
>
> Tests are essentially a type of exam. As with all examinations, they can be just right in difficulty, or they can be too easy or too difficult; in both of the latter cases, they give insufficient information on student progress. Tests may be *norm-referenced* or *criterion-referenced*.
>
> - *Norm-referenced* tests compare any given student's performance with that of the median student at the time the test was devised (for example);
> - *Criterion-referenced* tests measure whether the student has met the criterion of correctly solving certain specified problems.
>
> The international studies mentioned in this section are criterion-referenced in the sense that all tested students were given a set of questions agreed upon by an international committee of experts, and the percentage of correct answers per student was calculated. However, the comparison between countries could be regarded as a kind of norm-referencing if we regard some measure (say, the international average) as the basis of comparison. Norm-referenced tests are useless for intertemporal comparisons, unless we know how the norm itself has changed over time by criterion-referenced standards.
>
> Tests, *if properly chosen and used*, have three advantages:
>
> - As *diagnostic tools*, they indicate areas of strengths and weakness of performance; they enable students, teachers, and education policymakers to direct their efforts where they are needed the most.
> - As *tools of accountability*, tests and gains in test scores can (if the results are properly adjusted for other factors known to influence performance) help to determine whether the student, teacher, school, school district, and education system have done an adequate job.
> - As *tools of comparison* – again, if properly adjusted and used – tests enable us to know how well we are doing, compared with other countries, provinces, school boards, and schools.
>
> The main arguments of those opposing tests are as follows:
>
> - Tests measure inappropriate or irrelevant outcomes. The scope of education is far broader than what tests can measure.
> - Differences in test results are influenced by curriculum differences; students cannot be expected to know what they have not been taught; on the other hand, some of the things that students have learned in the classroom may not appear in the test.
> - Test results are often misused or misunderstood. Low test results may be the consequence of socio-economic factors, language difficulties, or family problems.
> - Tests, particularly those of large-scale multiple-choice, computer-evaluated studies, do not adequately measure higher-order skills.
> - Testing leads to "teaching to the test."
>
> Note that these criticisms are more valid against the wrong choice of tests or the misuse of their results than against testing *per se*.

perform above the bare minimum required to pass. If prospective employers – or even better, their trade associations – were to make it clear that they want to see secondary-school transcripts before hiring and that performing at, say, the 70-per-cent level in specified courses is a precondition, this would act as a powerful signal to young students heading for the labour market.

*Families, Friends, and Peers*

Self-motivation, and the

*motivation –> achievement –> motivation*

virtuous circle are perhaps the most powerful factors of educational success. But they are not the only ones, far from it.

The effect of the family and its socio-economic status on the achievement of children has been documented by innumerable studies. Experience in the United States has shown that children at risk – mostly those from visible minorities, the inner cities, or poor families – are often insufficiently prepared for school. Special programs like Head Start have proven useful to help such children to overcome the difficulties of the first few years of school.

The socio-economic status of parents is also reflected in the type of courses taken by their children. In Ontario, for example, the general understanding is that the so-called "advanced" programs are supposed to prepare students for universities; "general" programs, for community colleges; and "basic" programs, for entry into the labour force. The Toronto Board of Education reported that in 1987, 72 per cent of Grade 9 students were in advanced programs, 21 per cent in the general, and 7 per cent in the basic; 94 per cent of the students from a high socio-economic background were in advanced programs (and only 6 per cent in general and basic programs), but only 60 per cent of those from an unskilled background were in advanced programs. Eighty-five per cent of 15-year-old Toronto students from families whose head was a professional or a high-level manager completed eight or more credits, but only 59 per cent of those from families whose head fell into the "unskilled clerical and manual workers" category, did so. The reasons for these differences are manifold, and their possible interactions are not well known. Parents with a higher socio-economic status may influence their children to aim for more education. Being well-educated themselves, they may be better able to monitor, supervise, and if necessary, personally assist the progress of their offspring. They may be able to afford to hire tutors to improve their children's results. Their education consciousness may manifest itself by choosing to buy or rent housing in an area known for the high quality of its schools.

The effect of socio-economic status, important though it may be, must be qualified. After all, the above-mentioned Toronto study finds that 22 per cent of all students came from professional and higher-managerial families, whereas 72 per cent of the total student population were in advanced programs. Among the students of Chinese extraction, only 6 per cent came from professional/higher-managerial families; nevertheless, 89 per cent took advanced programs. The corresponding figures for Korean students were 10 per cent and 93 per cent, respectively. Clearly, in those instances, the cultural background and the traditional respect for parental wishes have a strong effect on achievement. *Education-conscious parents can have a major positive effect on the achievement of their children, irrespective of their socio-economic status.*

Family members can take helpful action early on. Reading to preschool children is one of the ways that parents can prepare children for school, and it has a lasting favourable effect. So does establishing conditions for regular meal- and bed-times and sufficient sleep, and other measures available to parents, such as the rationing of television watching. Systematic monitoring of homework is very important. Together with these must go a home atmosphere that makes it clear to children that it is not sufficient to pass but that they are expected to strive for the best they are capable of.

Societal ills have a major effect on student achievement. The Toronto study shows that 69 per cent of 15-year olds whose parents were both present in the home accumulated eight or more school credits. Of those whose mother only was present, some 59 per cent achieved the same result; of those whose father only was present, 54 per cent; and of those who lived without their parents, only 50 per cent. This is a clear indication of the effect of broken homes.

Classmates and class organization also have an impact, though it is difficult to assess. Young people differ widely in ability. Teachers maintain that academically homogeneous groups are easier to teach than heterogeneous ones. Essentially, all school systems eventually separate students by academic ability, but they do so in different ways. In some countries, like Japan, the students are sorted by school, and the more demanding and academically ambitious secondary schools accept only the best students; however, almost all Japanese teenagers do finish secondary school. Other countries – Germany, for instance – sort the students into schools that are of an avowedly academic or vocational character. The Canadian and U.S. systems essentially keep most students in the same type of school but sort them into what Ontario calls the advanced, general, and basic programs (or streams). The programs differ by academic content. The dilemma seems to be that here we have the worst of both worlds: the advanced program is too weak for the best students and too academic for potential drop-outs – but the drop-outs have few (and unattractive) vocational options.

Many educationists believe that streaming, and early streaming in particular, is harmful. They argue that those responsible for streaming often mis-group students. However, once a student has been assigned to, say, the general program, it is very unlikely that she/he could later move into the advanced one because of the slower academic pace of the general course; in practice the cumulative nature of education makes catching up to the advanced stream almost impossible. Students in the general and basic streams often regard themselves as stigmatized and are much more likely to drop out of school. This is a very different and much worse outcome than that of the German system, where the quality of vocational education is very high and where no stigma is attached to vocational schools and education. If grouping by ability is necessary, a system should be devised that does not deprive the students of their self-confidence and motivation. The literature on effective schools, to which we shall return later, also recommends that in each class there be a nucleus of students of at least average ability. This arrangement has a beneficial peer effect on all students (not only on the below-average ones).

*Teachers*

Although teachers play a vital role in the educational process, the quality of teachers and teaching is difficult to evaluate. That quality can be assessed, however, by the outcome of teaching – that is, by the progress made by the students, provided proper allowance is made for the differential conditions that make teaching easier or more difficult. For example, it is more difficult to teach the "language arts" (spelling, capitalization, punctuation, and usage) to allophone newcomers than to students whose home language is the same as the language of instruction. A class of eighth-graders whose numeracy is at the Grade 5 level is more difficult to bring up to grade level than one that has not fallen behind. The progress of learning is the criterion that measures good teaching, and regular testing can help to measure that progress.

Teachers themselves must be highly motivated in order to be able to motivate their students. While remuneration is only one source of teacher motivation, it is an important one; but there are other motivators of teachers. Teachers want, rightly, to be regarded and appreciated as professionals, but often they feel as mere cogs in a huge education machine in which they are the day-to-day decision makers in the classroom but have only limited influence on school-wide decisions and even less at the school-district level. The Edmonton School District data suggest that this tendency is found among elementary-school teachers, becomes more pronounced among junior-high teachers, and is strongest among senior-high teachers. For teachers to be expected to behave as professionals, they must be confident that they will be treated as professionals and that those who excel at teaching will be properly appreciated. Only too often, the way to promotion lies along the path of supervision of extracurricular programs and haphazard accumulation of postgraduate degrees that may or may not be relevant to the quality of teaching. Teachers who dislike teaching often strive for administrative positions. However, the ability to manage is also an important aspect of classroom teaching. Studies have repeatedly shown that the effective use of teaching time is a very important aspect of a teacher's talent. The more time is spent on administrative and disciplinary action, the less actual teaching can take place.

*Schools and School Resources*

Are some schools more effective than others? If so, what makes a school effective? The quality of facilities or the teacher/student ratio are not the sole factors affecting school effectiveness, which can be defined by such indicators as high scholastic attainment, desirable classroom behaviour, low absenteeism, positive attitudes to learning, continuation in education, satisfactory employment, and proper social functioning [see Rutter]. The inputs listed in Table 1 are often said to have a favourable effect on scholastic achievement. Yet a thorough review of 187 relevant studies devoted to examining the effects of one or more of these inputs shows no persuasive evidence confirming such effects. Note, however, that these results are based only on North American data. In addition, it cannot be inferred that the inputs shown in the table do not have a favourable effect on student achievement. It may well be that other, more important influences have not been included among the factors considered.

What are these influences? The current literature on effective schools summarizes these influences under the name of school *ethos* (spirit). It has been observed that successful schools share certain characteristics. Not all such schools necessarily possess all of these characteristics, nor do they possess them to the same degree. Nevertheless, there are enough similarities to enable us to draw conclusions.

**Table 1**

**Effects of selected input indicators on education-achievement test results, 187 studies, United States and Canada**

|  | Number of studies | Statistically significant effects Positive | Negative | Statistically insignificant |
|---|---|---|---|---|
| Teacher/pupil ratio | 152 | 14 | 13 | 125 |
| Teacher education | 113 | 8 | 5 | 100 |
| Teacher experience | 140 | 40 | 10 | 90 |
| Teacher salary | 69 | 11 | 4 | 54 |
| Expenditures/pupil | 65 | 13 | 3 | 49 |
| Administrative inputs | 61 | 7 | 1 | 53 |
| School facilities | 74 | 7 | 5 | 62 |

SOURCE  Based on Hanushek.

First, effective schools are clearly committed to high expectations and norms in matters of scholastic achievement and student behaviour, and teachers and students are well aware of this commitment. The teachers agree with the goals and plan courses collegially, and senior colleagues check and ensure that the school's policies are actually pursued. Academic expectations are high, but realistic.

Second, in effective schools a high percentage of classroom time is devoted to active teaching and to focusing the attention of the whole class on active learning. Relatively little time is spent on administration, discipline-oriented activities, setting up equipment, distributing books and papers, and so on. Homework is regularly set and expeditiously marked so as to give quick and constructive feedback to students. Good work is praised, rather than weak performance depreciated. In punctuality and reliability the teachers act as role models.

Third, the school environment encourages pupils to accept its school norms. The surroundings must be kept clean, attractive, and in good repair. This is more important than the age, size, or equipment of the school. Teachers must be accessible to students outside class time. Extracurricular activities with teachers help to establish a good relationship between staff and students. Giving students responsibility for certain class activities promotes their involvement and adoption of school values and norms.

In short, the school is a social organization, and as in all organizations, much depends on the chief executive officer – the principal. He or she must ensure that the whole team will work in a purposeful manner towards a goal jointly agreed to. This difficult task cannot be taught, and each principal must approach it in his or her own way. Many now believe that the best contribution that school boards and other education policymakers can make to higher educational standards is to set realistic targets and to assess and publicize the outcomes, while interfering as little as possible in the actual management of schools.

In the United States, there is evidence that those schools which have the most freedom and least bureaucratic interference (namely, private and religious schools) do best in increasing student achievement. Similarly, in Quebec – where private-school enrolment as a proportion of total enrolment is the highest in Canada – the achievement of students in private schools has consistently been higher than that of students in the public sector. In Ontario, Grade 8 private-school students taking part in the Second International Mathematics Study were, at the beginning of the school year, more than a full year ahead of their public-school counterparts.

While it is true that private schools, on the whole, draw their pupils from the higher socio-economic strata, results for U.S. religious schools show that the achievement gain is higher than one would expect on the basis of social background alone. This does not mean that all schools must be privatized. Rather, it suggests that achievement can be improved in the public-school system by reducing interference, increasing the principal's freedom, disseminating the results of assessments, and increasing parental freedom of choice among schools. Some of the pros and cons of the freedom to choose a school of one's preference are outlined in the box on p. 14.

*The Opportunity to Learn*

School is not the only source of learning for young people, but it is critical for the learning of mathematics and science. If these subjects are not included in curricula, students will obviously be unable to master them.

Scholastic achievement depends to a large extent on the "opportunity to learn" – a concept developed by the International Association for the Evaluation of Educational Achievement (IEA) and used in numerous studies. The IEA's test asks each teacher to respond to each test item in terms of whether or not his or her students have been exposed to the material needed to answer the question correctly.

One of the consistent findings of the IEA studies has been that "students who have greater opportunities to learn the knowledge and skills included on the achievement tests are likely to have higher levels of achievement" [Anderson and Postlethwaite, p. 76]. This held true not only in mathematics and science, but also in reading, writing and literacy.

As another review of the IEA results points out, "this general finding also appeals to common sense. Students tend to learn what they are taught" [Kifer, p. 55]. Why is it important to highlight this seemingly banal conclusion? Because there is growing evidence that the Canadian curriculum is less rich than those found in many industrialized countries (Figure 9).

Furthermore, there are not only important international differences. Within countries,

the differences between the classrooms in which the students had the most opportunity to learn and those in which they had the least was never less than 50 percent in any country. That is, in certain classrooms in each country students had an opportunity to learn the content associated with two or three times as many test items as did students in other

> ### Choosing the School of One's Preference
>
> In many countries, there is increasing support for allowing students and parents to choose their school within the public system. A payment from the appropriate educational authority, determined by a formula, would follow the student to the school of choice. The school would be free to spend the resulting budget as it pleases. Such a system would attempt to simulate the behaviour of the market in an industry presently characterized as quasi-monopolistic.
>
> Advantages
>
> - Parents and students could express their preferences and their view of the quality of schools.
> - Currently, such preferences are expressed by well-to-do parents who choose to buy or rent housing in areas with good schools or send their children to private schools. The proposed system would extend this freedom of choice to the less well-off.
> - It would force the good schools to maintain – and the less good ones, to upgrade – the quality of instruction.
> - It would encourage schools to develop a set of values – the school ethos – conducive to learning.
>
> Disadvantages
>
> - Good schools would attract strong students – and weak schools, the weaker students – hereby widening disparities in school quality.
> - Areas with a low tax base could not compete for resources, unless given additional funds by the financing authorities.
> - It is the weak student who needs the most resources.
> - The community ties fostered by the common school would be loosened.
>
> Problems
>
> - In case of freedom of choice, should the payment follow the child even to private schools?
> - If a school proves particularly popular, will the central authorities provide the funds needed for expansion? Conversely, will the authorities allow particularly weak schools to go bankrupt?
> - Will the authorities allow new schools to enter the system?
> - Is there much justification for freedom of choice if a common curriculum is imposed?
> - Can decentralized schools operate in a freedom-of-choice environment as long as the salaries of teachers are set by collective bargaining, involving a strongly centralized union?
> - Unless a central authority provides the correct information, how could parents make an appropriate choice among schools?
> - Should schools that take less-able or socially disadvantaged children receive higher payments?

classrooms. The implications of this finding . . . are straightforward. To the extent that the opportunity to learn influences student achievement, students in these different classrooms will perform differently [Sellin and Anderson, p. 176].

One of the most damning arguments against the practice of "tracking" or "streaming" is that many youngsters are incorrectly assigned to a lower stream and are then intellectually malnourished because they are "fed" much less than they are able to absorb. Thus the classification into a lower track becomes a completely unjustified self-fulfilling prophecy. Less harm is done by keeping the "true" slow learners in a program with richer content, even if they cannot absorb all that is offered.

In every subject, the opportunity to learn is influenced by the time devoted to teaching the subject. If we wish to improve achievement in the subjects deemed essential, it will be necessary to impose strict limits on the time devoted to elective subjects. This does not mean that curricula must be identical for every student, but it does mean that each student should spend most of the instruction time on his or her core subjects.

One would think that the opportunity to learn a subject is favourably influenced by the length of the school year, the length of the school day, and the proportion of time devoted to that subject. The fragmentary international evidence available suggests that there is indeed a systematic correlation between the length of the school year and higher educational achievement; however, longer school days and greater amounts of time devoted to a given subject do not have a direct recognizable effect on achievement – at least within the limits practised in the school systems of the industrialized countries. What conclusions can we draw from this surprising finding?

Education and Training in Canada    15

**Figure 9**

Correlation between the opportunity to learn and achievement in mathematics among secondary-level students in selected industrialized countries,[1] early 1980s

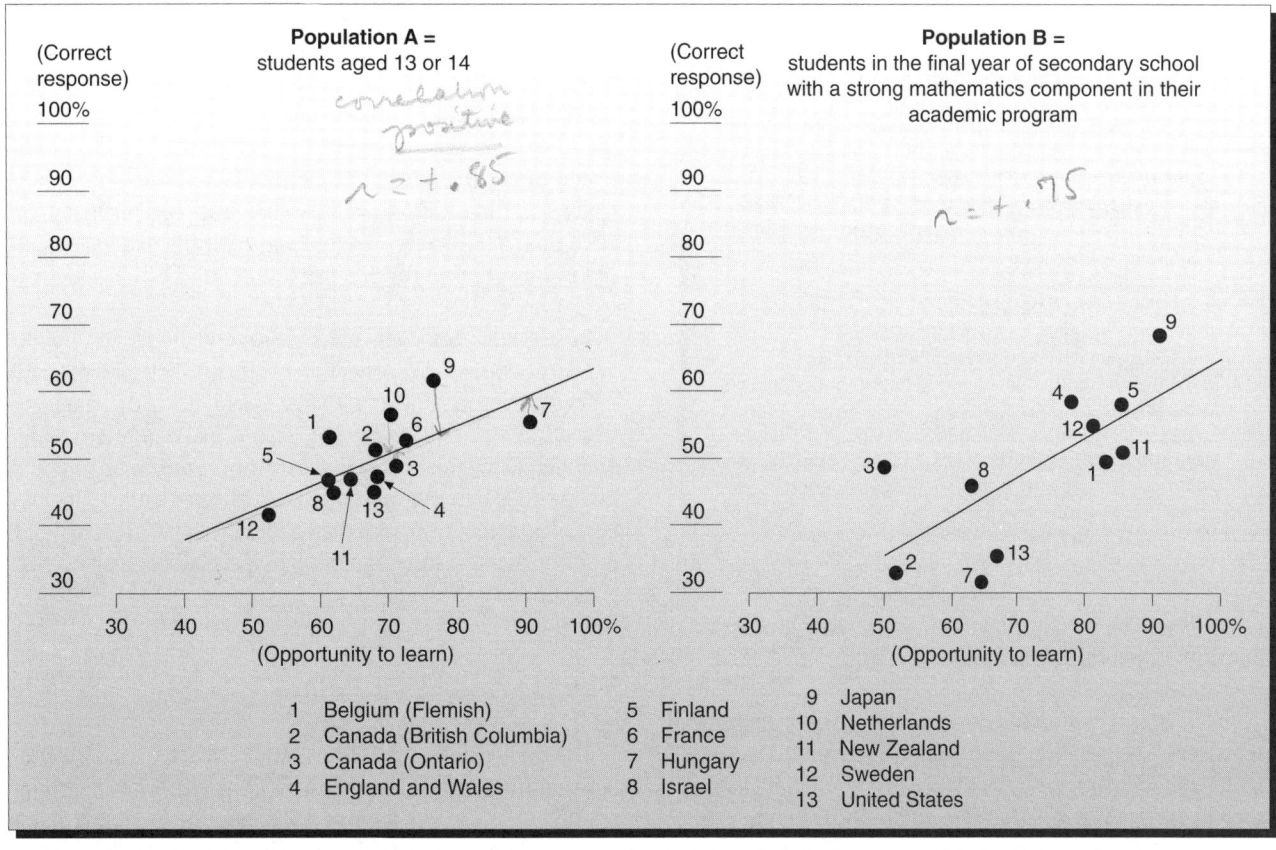

1  The dots show, for each country, the correlation between the exposure of students to mathematical concepts and the level of correct responses to a test of the knowledge of mathematics.
SOURCE  Estimates by the Economic Council, based on the findings of the Second International Mathematics Study (see Robitaille and Garden).

The *IEA Classroom Environment Study* concludes that the effective use of available time for learning ("time on task") is at least as important as the assigned amount of time. While there is virtually no valid international information available on the effective use of assigned time, we know that it is higher in those *schools* which are characterized by a strong academic ethos. We may conjecture that the longer school year is an indicator of those *countries* which are more education-conscious. The longer school year is not the *cause* of higher achievement, but both are reflections or results of the importance that society attaches to educational achievement. The longer school year would not, by itself, lead to higher achievement, unless it were accompanied by a better use of time during the school day. We believe that improving the use of time during the school day should have priority over the lengthening of the school year (see box on p. 16).

*Summary*

Our education system has many strengths. Its accessibility is high, and it provides good education in the first four years of schooling. Academic admission standards to the teaching profession are much more demanding than they were in the past or are currently in the United States.

Nevertheless, we have no grounds for complacency. Some 30 per cent of our young people do not complete secondary school. The achievement record of secondary-school leavers is not as good as that of students in lower grades, and it is outright disappointing in mathematics and science. In addition, there are troubling differences across provinces in matters of scholastic achievement – gaps that cannot be explained away by differences in educational spending per

> **Some Research Issues for the Future**
>
> There are substantial gaps in our knowledge about Canadian educational achievement and how to improve it. Filling in these gaps is an urgent research priority.
>
> - There is little reliable information on valid interprovincial comparisons.
> - Little is known about the quality of teachers.
> - Data on the *level* of interprovincial achievement do not permit measurement of the *improvement* accomplished during the academic year and do not make allowance for factors that may have a crucial influence on achievement, such as parental socio-economic status and language in the home.
> - Is there a trade-off between equity and achievement in streaming? What is the best compromise?
> - Is there a trade-off between cost and class size?
> - Is there sufficient empirical study before pedagogic reforms are introduced?
> - A large-scale longitudinal study tracking a sufficiently large sample from preschool years through primary, secondary, and postsecondary schooling is needed.

student. Nor do we find signs of improved educational achievement over the past 25 years.

Education is a cumulative process. Improving the standards of secondary-school graduates requires careful preparation and the setting of ambitious standards throughout the full period of elementary and secondary education. This has many implications. In particular, the students' self-motivation is an essential factor. Motivated students will rise to challenges, particularly when exposed to a school environment that is demanding but also appreciative of good effort. This holds true for the academic as well as the vocational type of education.

Effective schools can contribute greatly to student achievement by creating a learning ethos that invests effort and achievement with prestige. The school is more likely to achieve this if it has a substantial degree of autonomy, giving the principal and the senior teaching staff the possibility to plan the curriculum in a collaborative manner. This requires a collegial relationship and a sense of community within the staff, and also a reasonable degree of staff stability. Curriculum planning should centre on high expectations and clear goals in a limited number of key subjects, with very few electives.

Academic success depends on orderly and disciplined classrooms. Keeping students actively involved in learning and minimizing the waste of time by administrative tasks, disciplining, and public announcements, increases the opportunity to learn. Frequent feedback from teachers to students is a strong motivator, particularly if the emphasis is on praise for good work rather than ridicule or punishment for errors. Teachers are also role models: their knowledge, enthusiasm, conscientious work, sensitivity, and appreciative feedback are all-important ingredients of the ethos of effective schools. The principal and the teachers create the social framework for educational success. But as in every social system, there is a need for accountability and monitoring of achievement. They provide the necessary conditions for diagnosing weaknesses and for building on strengths. Intelligently devised and carefully evaluated testing is a useful tool for this task.

In addition, however, parental involvement and support is also necessary. Students must feel that their parents, and indeed society as a whole, assign the highest importance to education and that doing the acceptable minimum is not enough. They must learn that effort is appreciated and that doing one's best is the source both of satisfaction and success. The effect of parents' attitudes on the achievement of their children is greater and more important than that of their socio-economic status.

## The Learning Continuum

The traditional model, in which "schooling" and "work" were quite distinct activities, is obsolete. The "learning continuum" conveys the notion of learning as a continuing process from early childhood education through elementary and secondary schooling to the array of learning activities of adulthood. In particular, it emphasizes the need, in the information age, for continual upgrading. Thus, today, one encounters expressions such as "lifelong learning," "recurrent education," or "further education and training."

In the new model, then, learning is an integral dimension of work. This can be seen clearly in Figure 10, where the labour market is depicted as the backdrop against which learning takes place. People move constantly between work and learning institutions; in fact, a great many participate in both simultaneously. As the authors of a recent study stated, "a surprisingly high proportion of both high-school and university graduates in our samples remained in the educational system after graduation. What distinguishes graduates in the 1980s from those in earlier decades are these diverse combinations of education and work" [Krahn and Lowe, pp. 7-8]. To be able to continue to learn, of course, people must have a solid base of "foundation" skills on which to build – hence our repeated emphasis on literacy and numeracy, and on the other basic skills provided in the elementary and secondary systems.

**Figure 10**
**The learning continuum**

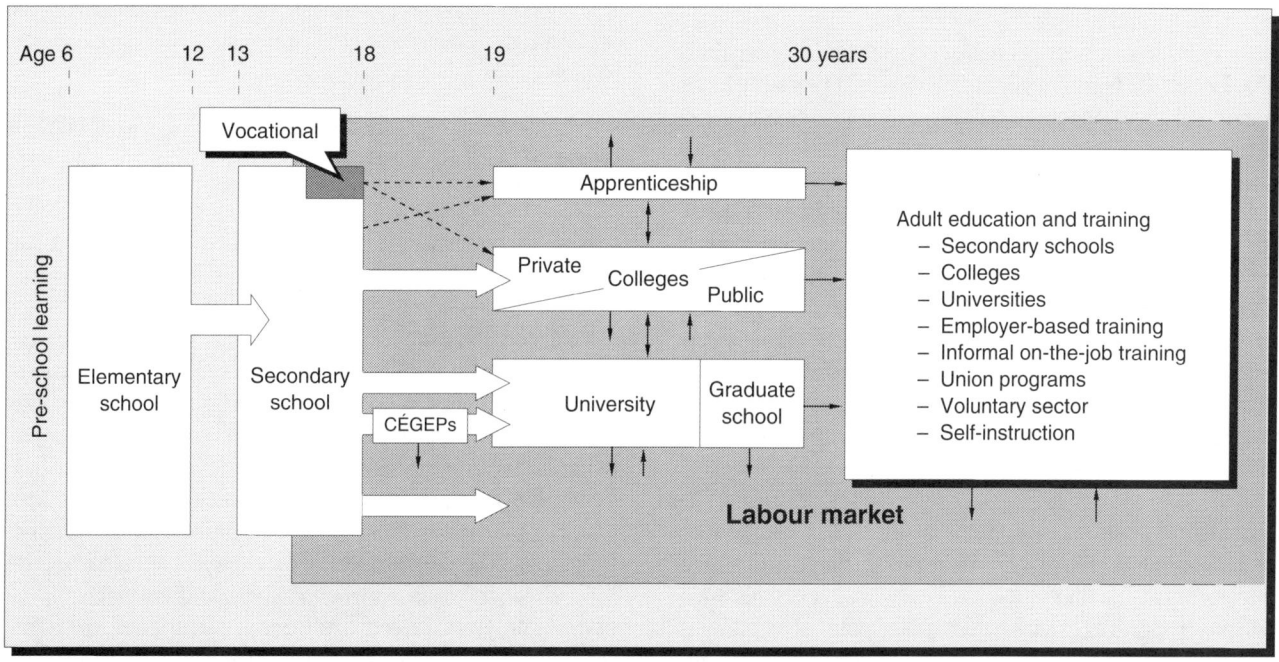

Vocational programs – our main focus here – are of great importance because of their direct implications for competitiveness and because demographic trends in the labour force put a premium on adult learning. But they also play a critical role in fostering the goal of "coherence," introduced earlier. The clear transmission of signals from industry about skill requirements, and the education and training systems' ability to respond, are especially relevant in the case of vocational programs.

Such learning activities are carried out in a variety of ways – secondary schools, colleges, universities, and private career colleges; with government help, through training and apprenticeship programs; by employers, through formal training programs or more informal on-the-job training; and through industry associations, trade-union programs, and programs of the voluntary sector.

These learning avenues are depicted in Figure 10. Two examples of lack of coherence are illustrated in the figure. First, the broken lines from secondary-school programs to the postsecondary apprenticeship stream and from vocational secondary school to college reflect our conclusion that there is insufficient "articulation" – a lack of clear pathways, linkages, and accreditation between these various elements of the continuum. The same can be said of transfers between apprenticeship programs, colleges, and universities, as indicated by the broken two-way arrows. (Not seen in the figure, however, are some innovative ways of promoting vocational learning at various levels – namely, partnerships, dealt with later on.)

A second feature of the learning continuum is that there is a great deal of movement between the labour market and the learning avenues. The short vertical arrows indicate this continual process of dropping in and dropping out. In fact, of course, at any moment, millions of Canadians work and take educational or training courses simultaneously. While this may seem reassuring, our work suggests that, too often, the process is haphazard. Indeed, one of the key observations here is that Canada lacks institutional mechanisms to ensure that labour-market signals are clearly transmitted and correctly read by individuals and the learning institutions.

*Vocational Education in Secondary Schools*

One of our principal conclusions is that the options for the nonacademic student have been neglected and that the general disrepute in which vocational programs are held is damaging. Partly, the problem is one of misplaced expectations: most parents, and the students themselves, aspire to prestigious positions via university or college – often with little comprehension of what this actually entails. Many youngsters do, in fact, ultimately find their niche in well-paying trades and technical positions after more or less fruitlessly dabbling in postsecondary courses and/or part-time jobs. Under the German system, they would probably have found well-paid jobs more quickly and at less cost to society.

A recent research paper by Employment and Immigration Canada on secondary-school vocational education reviews course offerings in the various provinces and identifies a handful of very good programs, but concludes that they are far too few and do not reach nearly enough students. According to the study, while every province except Newfoundland has vocational programs in secondary school, only about 10 per cent of Canadian students are enrolled in them.

Data on vocational programs at the secondary-school level are poor. However, it appears that in Ontario enrolments in "technological studies" – which include such subjects as drafting, construction, and electrical and television repairs – have declined as a proportion of overall enrolments during the period 1985-88. A similar decline has been observed for Alberta in the same period. Particularly striking is the case of Quebec, where the proportion of students in vocational programs leading to certification declined from 18.0 per cent in 1976-77 to 4.6 per cent in 1988-89. In the Quebec case, however, vocational programs at the secondary-school level have been substantially altered recently, and the 1991 estimate of the proportion of students in such courses is 25 per cent. Further efforts to improve these programs involve collaboration between the Ministry of Education and the Ministry of Industry, Commerce and Technology, which has identified shortages of special skills.

Why do secondary-school vocational programs have a poor image? A number of reasons have been suggested:

– the programs tend to be geared towards high-risk students and/or low achievers;

– the staff of vocational schools frequently do not have advanced formal qualifications;

– postsecondary institutions often do not accept vocational subjects as credits;

– the formal links between secondary-school vocational programs and apprenticeship programs are uneven and incomplete (although new initiatives are under way in some provinces);

– a secondary school's success is often judged by how well it prepares students for university rather than by how well it prepares them for the labour market;

– Canadian society ascribes a lower socio-economic status to blue-collar jobs;

– guidance counsellors estimate that some 95 per cent of Grade 10 students aspire to university entrance – an unrealistic expectation that is often reinforced by parents;

– career counsellors are frequently ill-informed about the content and prospects of the jobs of the 1990s.

That said, there are some encouraging signs that increased attention is being paid to vocational programs by provincial governments. Ontario's "Skill OK" program to promote skilled occupations as desirable career goals is an example of an attempt to address the perception problem. British Columbia's "Passport to Apprenticeship" program and Ontario's Secondary School Workplace Apprenticeship Program (SSWAP) are specific examples of attempts to provide direct linkages between schools and regular apprenticeship programs. Recent reforms to vocational education in Quebec involve a systematic review of program effectiveness and efforts to increase vocational enrolments by improving the image of vocational offerings. For example, there is a proposal to eliminate the secondary-school vocational diploma, which has been associated with low achievers and high-risk students, to review admission criteria, and to recognize relevant experience acquired outside the school.

Nevertheless, more must be done to improve the image of vocational education and training. In particular, where secondary-school-level apprenticeships are offered, they should be coordinated with the regular postsecondary apprenticeship system. At the same time, course offerings should be geared to occupations that closely reflect the emerging occupational structure of the dominant service economy.

## Colleges

In Canada, approximately 200 publicly funded community colleges and *collèges d'enseignement général et professionnel (CÉGEPS)* serve a large and growing student body in a wide variety of vocational courses. Enrolment in the system expanded rapidly in the late 1970s and early 1980s, levelled off later in that decade, and is now rising again. Of the 321,000 full-time and 187,000 part-time students, about two thirds are in career programs (as opposed to university transfer programs).

One curious aspect of the system is that, during a period of rapid technological change, enrolment in technology courses has actually declined in recent years. For Canada as a whole, enrolments in engineering and applied science as a proportion of all enrolments fell noticeably (by 25 per cent) between 1983 and 1989. And in Quebec's CÉGEP system, the proportion of vocational enrolment declined by 14 per cent during the 1980s. Enrolments in certain CÉGEP programs fell dramatically between 1984 and 1988: by 47 per cent in electronics, for example; and by 53 per cent in informatics.

Why did these phenomena occur? In part, they may reflect those same factors which underlie the poor image of vocational education generally, and technological studies in particular, at the secondary-school level. A study of the situation in Ontario colleges points to reduced numbers of secondary-school leavers qualified in mathematics and science. More disturbing, however, is the finding that the marketing efforts of Ontario colleges themselves failed to attract enough prospective students.

The most recent figures suggest that the trend may have bottomed out. For Canada as a whole, the proportion of enrolments in engineering and applied sciences remained at 22.7 per cent between 1988-89 and 1989-90, after having decreased by 4.3 percentage points since 1985-86. In Quebec, the proportion of enrolments in vocational programs rose by 13 per cent in 1990-91, while enrolments in the physics technician programs rose by 16 per cent.

However, the colleges do strive constantly to respond to the needs of students and of local employers – a process that is epitomized by Vision 2000, Ontario's recent massive review of the mandate of the college system. But given labour-market realities, the colleges must seek new, innovative ways to contribute to the planning, design, and implementation of vocational courses, in direct collaboration with local employers and the wider community. There are, of course, many examples of such collaborative efforts already at play – among others that of Mohawk College in Hamilton, which offers numerous courses tailored to the needs of local employers and is now experimenting with "distance" education (e.g., courses delivered by television or through audio or video cassettes, etc.) to deliver vocational programs. The British Columbia Institute of Technology has developed a training partnership agreement with B.C. Tel that explicitly recognizes the company's in-house training by conferring credits towards four of the college's certificate programs.

In Quebec, some 15 CÉGEPs provide courses designed to impart the latest skills and techniques pertinent to local industries. These range from fibre optics and laser technology in the association between Bombardier and the La Pocatière CÉGEP, to mineral technology in the asbestos industry, and fashion design at Collège La Salle, a private institution. What is especially important, in these Quebec examples, is the role of private firms. Local businesses transfer recent technology to the colleges by providing machinery, equipment, and staff; and the colleges train technicians to work in the local industries. The bulk of the costs of the public college system are usually covered by the province; typically, less than 10 per cent is raised from fees. But in Quebec's industry/college partnerships, 50 per cent of the project costs, on average, is covered by the participating enterprises.

These programs cater to regular CÉGEP students working towards the *diplôme d'études collégiales*. Colleges in Quebec and Ontario also sell custom-designed vocational courses to local employers. Students in these courses are usually adults. In some cases, the cost of these courses is partly borne by Employment and Immigration Canada (EIC). Unfortunately, there is as yet insufficient data to evaluate such courses.

Clearly, these are exemplary cases within the public college system. But problems remain. While, again, there are exceptions – Quebec and British Columbia are examples – "articulation" is often one of those problems. That is, preparation for, and transfer of credits to, university is too often unsystematic. Hence, options and pathways are curtailed.

Even less is known about the burgeoning private-sector vocational system, though an attempt is made here to provide some basic descriptive information from a variety of sources. As Table 2 shows, there are about 1,000 private colleges offering postsecondary career training in trades and in technical and business subjects in small and large communities across the country. Of these, about 350 are either members of a provincial association and/or are designated as institutions eligible for the Canada Student Loan Plan. They are licensed, registered, and controlled by provincial authorities, which regulate curricula, set requirements for teachers' credentials and student outcomes, and control tuition fees. Because these institutions focus primarily on preparing students for successful employment, their placement record is an important criterion in assessing their performance. And while fees may be considered relatively high, private-college students will typically graduate in a significantly shorter period than their community-college counterparts, so that forgone earnings are minimized.

Overall, across Canada, the number of institutions, the range of courses offered, and enrolments have grown

**Table 2**

**Data on private career colleges, Canada, 1989**

|  | Designated[1] | Total |
|---|---|---|
| Number of colleges | 350 | 1,000 |
| Number of employees | 5,000 | 9,000 |
| Number of students | 75,000 | 140,000 |
|  | ($ million) | |
| Total tuition revenue | 233 | 380 |
| Labour expense | 110 | 175 |
| Estimated corporate taxes | 6 | 10 |

1 Institutions that belong to a provincial association of private colleges and/or that have been designated by the federal government as institutions whose students are eligible for Canada Student Loans assistance.

SOURCE Data supplied by the Newfoundland Career Academy.

substantially in recent years. Growth has been most rapid in the two provinces where private colleges are the most prominent – British Columbia (with nearly half of all private career colleges in the country) and Ontario (with about one fourth of the total). Between 1986 and 1990, enrolments increased by over 50 per cent in British Columbia and by almost one third in Ontario. The typical school is quite small and specialized. Courses in business, technology, and trades represent the bulk of enrolments, though community service, modelling, and cosmetology also attract relatively large numbers of students.

There is very little information available concerning the relative performance of public and private vocational colleges, and comparisons must be interpreted with caution. Private colleges have higher per-course fees, but course duration is shorter there than in public colleges, so that income forgone is less; in addition, private colleges boast a significantly higher placement rate. Private-college fees for "technology and trades" courses are typically of the order of $3,000, while community-college students across the country face yearly fees for science and technology courses of about $1,000. In Quebec, the CÉGEPs are free, but a prominent private college in Montreal charges close to $2,000 a year for technology courses.

Clearly, a great deal of further research is required to assess the relative performance of public and private colleges. What, for example, is the relative degree of satisfaction of the respective student populations? Initial placement success is important, but what of subsequent employment experience? What is the relative quality of the occupations to which the two sets of graduates may aspire? And how do employers judge the relative quality of graduates of public and private institutions performing similar jobs? Such questions should, we believe, be a research priority, since cost effectiveness is a major challenge for the Canadian vocational sector.

*Apprenticeship*

A number of recent reports, including those of the Ontario Premier's Council and of the Canadian Labour Market and Productivity Centre's Task Force on Apprenticeship, have called for reform of the apprenticeship system. They suggest ways and means to integrate more efficiently the respective responsibilities of the private sector and the federal and provincial governments, to reform funding arrangements for apprenticeship training, to promote national standards and mobility for those who complete an apprenticeship program, and to increase the participation rates of women and other groups. Our research, which is based on the analysis of the data from the recent National Apprenticeship Survey (conducted by Statistics Canada on behalf of Employment and Immigration Canada) plus administrative records, complements earlier findings and casts further light on certain features of the existing apprenticeship system. The key stylized facts emerging from the National Apprenticeship Survey are shown in the box. In particular, we note that Canadian apprentices are old, by international standards; in addition, only 12 per cent of total enrolments in 1986-87 were female, and only 41 per cent of program completers were awarded an interprovincial standards certificate. Previous trade-related experience seems to contribute to success, but over one third of graduates who had such experience received no credit for it.

*National Standards and Costs*

Before discussing our findings, two issues are worthy of consideration. The first has to do with national standards and mobility. The diversity of training programs is a major concern to both employers and apprentices. Since the system allows the provinces to develop their own training programs independently, consistency in program quality throughout the country has been elusive. Employers have few guarantees of consistent standards; and for the apprentices themselves the system inevitably limits mobility.

The Interprovincial Standards Program (also known as the Red Seal program) was established in 1959 to promote national standards in provincial apprenticeship training programs. In practice, however, the number of occupational trades granting Red Seals to more than 50 per cent of their graduates have been few.

### Highlights of Results from the National Apprenticeship Survey

**Good News**

- 12 months after graduation, 96 per cent of graduates worked in their apprenticed trades.
- 81 per cent of the leavers who worked in trade-related jobs found the skills learned mostly or all relevant.
- People with trade-related experience prior to apprenticeship had better chances to complete all program requirements.

**Bad News**

- Only 12 per cent of registrants were female.
- The average age of program leavers was 27 years.
- 33 to 42 per cent of the graduates had some prior trade-related training but did not receive credits towards program requirements.

**News**

- 12 months after leaving the programs, 50 per cent of the non-completers worked in their apprenticed trades.
- 12 per cent of the leavers who worked in non-trade-related jobs found the skills learned mostly or all relevant.
- 13 per cent of the leavers experienced difficulty in finding employers to accept them as apprentices.

SOURCE  Data from Statistics Canada's National Apprenticeship Survey, 1989/90, and estimates by the Economic Council of Canada.

---

Second, comparisons are often made with Germany's much-vaunted "dual" system of apprenticeship. Table 3 shows the smaller proportion of Canadian workers in apprenticeship and the greater relative cost of the Canadian system. The apprentices themselves bear part of the cost in terms of potential earnings forgone. And there is a complex division of funding responsibilities between federal and provincial governments. Finally, it costs a Canadian firm much more money ($170,000 versus $51,000) to train an apprentice because the apprenticeship term is longer in this country and because the average age of Canadian trainees is higher. Many Canadian apprentices are old enough to have families to support and mortgage payments to meet. Another factor contributing to higher costs is the fact that legislated minimum-wage rates for Canadian apprentices tend to be much higher than those paid to young German apprentices.

*Responsiveness of the Apprenticeship System*

From the existing employment data, we notice that most of the employment growth in the Canadian economy in recent years has been in services. During the period 1967-89, the annual average employment growth rates in major sectors were:

| | |
|---|---|
| manufacturing | 1.0 per cent |
| construction | 1.9 per cent |
| "dynamic" services | 3.2 per cent |
| traditional services | 3.2 per cent |
| nonmarket services | 3.3 per cent |

### Table 3
**Apprenticeship statistics, Canada and West Germany, 1987**

| | Canada | West Germany |
|---|---|---|
| | (Millions) | |
| Population | 25.6 | 61.2 |
| Labour force | 12.8 | 29.4 |
| | (Thousands) | |
| Apprentices | | |
| Total number | 122 | 1,800 |
| | (Per cent) | |
| As a proportion of the labour force | 0.95 | 6.1 |
| | (Years) | |
| Average age of apprentices | 26 | 17 |
| Length of apprenticeship | 4-5 | 2-3 |
| | ($ thousand) | |
| Cost of apprenticeship[1] | 170 | 51 |
| Apprenticeship wages[1] | 120 | 25 |

1 The apprenticeship programs examined here lasted five years in Canada and three and a half years in West Germany. The cost of apprenticeship includes the wages of apprentices.
SOURCE  Based on data from Siemens Electric Limited, from Statistics Canada, and from the OECD.

(Dynamic services include transport and communications; utilities; finance, insurance and real estate; and business services.)

Throughout the 1980s, however, more than 90 per cent of the occupations covered by apprenticeship pertained to manufacturing, construction, or traditional services. Should one conclude that the apprenticeship system is oriented to employment in shrinking sectors or in sectors that, while growing, are growing slowly? Are knowledge- and technology-intensive occupations unsuitable for apprenticeship? Clearly, the system is very highly concentrated. While some 290 occupations are, in principle, apprenticeable, fewer than one third actually had registered apprentices in 1987 – at a time when employers registered vacancies in close to 400 occupational categories.

Our research also tested the responsiveness issue by looking at how well the supply of completing apprentices in various occupations responded to demand conditions. Of the 84 occupations considered, correlations with general labour-market demand conditions for the period 1974-87 revealed only two occupations – service-station attendants and radio/television technicians – for which responsiveness could be regarded as "good," according to our criteria. The more specific correlations between the supply of graduates and job vacancies in specific occupations showed four good responses – hairdressers, telecommunications electricians, heavy-equipment operators, and insulators. The majority of cases were "bad" or, in particular, "unrelated." The analysis suggests that little attempt was made to synchronize the supply of apprentices with the demand of employers for occupational workers. Here, we believe, is an example of a lack of coherence. If policymakers expect apprenticeship training to play a major role in the labour market, then the demand for, and supply of, apprentices must be better planned and integrated.

## Continuous Skill Upgrading

Perhaps the most underrated form of continuous learning is informal self-instruction by individual persons. The widespread acquisition of basic computer skills by a large segment of the population in the past decade testifies to this. But there is an array of lifelong learning possibilities, as shown in Figure 10; new information from Statistics Canada on Canadian adults taking training or educational courses is shown in the box.

Clearly, continuous upgrading is a pursuit undertaken by large numbers of Canadian workers. But just what are the skills demanded in the rapidly evolving industrial world? The articulation of such needs is a crucial component of coherence, since clear signals are necessary for institutions and individuals to respond appropriately.

---

**Continuing Education and Adult Training in Canada**

A survey of adult Canadians conducted between December 1989 and November 1990 indicated that:

- 1.4 million of the people surveyed were enrolled in full-time courses;
- 3.4 million were in short-term or part-time programs;
- 173,000 were in apprenticeship or other full-time training programs organized by an employer;
- management and business courses were the most popular for both full-time and part-time learners;
- for part-time, the most popular programs were engineering, applied science, technology, and trades;
- some 42 per cent of the adults taking courses were enrolled full-time;
- 84 per cent of short-term and part-time students were employed;
- improving job skills or career prospects were cited as the motives of 89 per cent of full-time trainees and 75 per cent of short-term or part-time participants;
- as far as employer support is concerned, while 42 per cent of part-time students had tuition fees reimbursed, the figure for full-time trainees was only 3 per cent;
- time off was given to 22 per cent of part-time students and 2 per cent of full-time students.

SOURCE  Statistics Canada, Adult Education and Training Survey, preliminary results published in *Perspectives*, Autumn 1991, p. 58.

---

## Skill Needs and Employers' Responses

The problems of illiteracy, innumeracy, and lack of other basic skills are frequently cited as barriers to productivity increase and effective human-resource development. Certainly, there is evidence that these problems are widespread. A recent Conference Board survey [see DesLauriers] indicates that 70 per cent of Canadian businesses considered illiteracy a problem for their operations. Over 30 per cent of respondents indicated that literacy deficits impeded general training and/or the acquisition of new and advanced skills. Surprisingly, given the widespread nature of these problems, only 24 per cent had a specific policy to deal with them. However, 36 per cent of responding firms indicated that they had a pre-employment test to screen out illiterates and innumerates.

Next, it appears that employers experience difficulties in obtaining certain technical skills. A telephone survey of 822 high-tech firms during the summer of 1989 revealed pervasive staffing problems. Fifty-five per cent reported problems in recruiting and retaining professional, scientific, and technical staff; 34 per cent reported similar problems with regard to skilled labour. Some 65 per cent said they expected such difficulties to persist; 21 per cent expected the problems to worsen. Many employers laid some of the blame for this on the education system. For example, some 24 per cent found universities less than adequate in preparing individuals for the work force, and 58 per cent found the elementary and secondary schools lacking in this regard.

Almost half of high-tech firms in Canada have formal training programs. Nearly all large firms (those with more than 1,000 employees) have such programs, but only 64 per cent of medium-sized companies (between 100 and 999 employees) and 37 per cent of small companies do so. Moreover, a disturbing finding is that most high-tech training goes to employees who are already highly skilled; the most common kind of training among the reporting firms was for professional and management categories.

Industry representatives have not been hesitant, of late, to express dissatisfaction with the quality of skills brought to the workplace by new entrants. But precise statements about the level and mix of foundation skills that they expect to find in new recruits are all too rare, especially at the secondary level. Students and teachers find it difficult to respond appropriately if there is uncertainty about employers' expectations. That is precisely the rationale for improving coherence through partnerships, as discussed later on.

*Employer-Based Training*

Given these perceptions of skill needs, just what is the extent of training in industry, and where is it performed? Some insights can be gained from recent evidence provided by Statistics Canada's Human Resource Training and Development (HRTD) survey. The major conclusion to be drawn from this body of data is the difference between very small firms (those with fewer than 10 employees) and large ones (with over 1,000 employees).

From Figure 11 it may be seen that small firms constitute the vast majority of all firms in Canada and represent, thereby, the majority of trainers. However, *proportionately* their training effort is inferior: only 27 per cent of small firms conduct training, while fully 76 per cent of large firms do so. In most major industry sectors, about one third of companies offer training, though the proportion in construction is less than one fourth; in food production, it is about one sixth. As for the motivation for training, a surprisingly small proportion of small companies (fewer than one fourth) identified new technologies as a source of skill needs.

As far as spending is concerned, it is disturbing to find that only 15 per cent of Canadian companies have a spe-

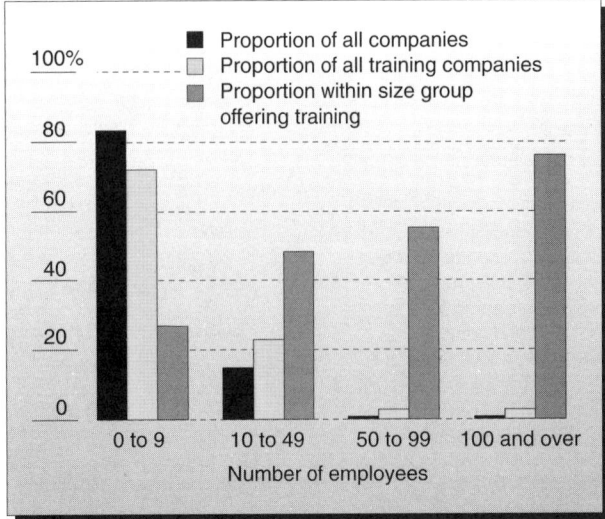

**Figure 11**

**Importance of training, by company size, Canada, 1987**

SOURCE   Based on data from Statistics Canada, "Distribution Report, Human Resource Training and Development Survey," Ottawa, 1990.

cial budget for training; there is a wide gap between small firms and large corporations in that respect: only 13 per cent of small firms had a training budget, but the figure was 59 per cent for large firms. And large firms, despite being relatively few in number (1 per cent overall), account for 45 per cent of all training expenditures.

Were their efforts successful? Curiously, a larger proportion of small than of large training companies think they met their training needs. The reasons cited by the firms that did not meet those needs are instructive. Most surprisingly, very large firms cited a combination of resource deficiencies (such as limited resources, courses, and training facilities) much more frequently than did small firms (63 per cent, as opposed to 54 per cent). Small firms were more prone to cite inadequacies in government programs (25 per cent versus 21 per cent for large firms). In fact, small firms tend to use government programs rather less than very large firms, and their dissatisfaction with government programs is reflected in the figures of Table 4. While, somewhat surprisingly, all firms were familiar with at least one program of EIC's Canadian Jobs Strategy, 58 per cent of small companies (against 40 per cent of large firms) said they would not use any program again.

In sum, the message is clear. Small firms undertake relatively less training of their own volition. But government

**Table 4**

**Awareness/usage of Employment and Immigration Canada's "Canadian Jobs Strategy" program among Canadian firms, by size, 1987**

|  | Very small firms[1] | Very large firms[2] | All firms |
|---|---|---|---|
|  | \multicolumn{3}{c}{(Per cent)} |  |
| Familiar with at least one program | 100 | 100 | 100 |
| Participated in at least one program | 49 | 65 | 53 |
| Did not participate in any program | 51 | 35 | 47 |
| Would use again at least one program | 42 | 60 | 44 |
| Would not use any program again | 58 | 40 | 56 |

1 Fewer than 10 employees.
2 More than 1,000 employees.
SOURCE Based on Statistics Canada's Human Resource Training and Development survey.

programs intended to make good this deficiency have not been embraced with enthusiasm.

Statistics Canada's HRTD survey and others of a similar nature have been criticized for using too narrow a definition of training. It has been argued, in particular, that statistics on the training effort of Canadian business (of small firms, especially) would be much more accurate if informal training were taken into account. A 1988 survey by the Canadian Federation of Independent Business concluded that small firms invest both time and money in training and that 70 per cent provide some form of training to their work force.

Clearly, it would be useful to take account systematically of this very important informal component when assessing the overall training effort of small firms, in particular. A few comments are in order, however. First, questions can be raised about the quality and effectiveness of this type of informal training. Second, to say that when informal training is taken into account the small business sector "looks better" is to suggest – inaccurately – that, *proportionately*, small firms do a great deal more informal training than large ones. Third, and similarly, to say that Canadian business would rank relatively better internationally if informal training were taken into account is to suggest – again, contrary to the evidence available – that Canadians do proportionately more of it than do their trading partners.

*A Role for "Distance" Education*

In the matter of continuous skill upgrading, there is scope for major contributions to the learning continuum through the alternate delivery mechanisms represented by "distance" education. The potential of this vehicle in the field of vocational education and training, in particular, is enormous and, as yet, largely untapped. Interactive training and the provision of labour-market information and career counselling through the electronic medium could do much to enhance coherence. More detailed information about the role of distance education in Canada is contained in our research report, which describes the technologies, as well as their scope and potential.

We note with interest that TV Ontario recently submitted a proposal for an "Ontario Skills Training Channel" – a 24-hour television channel that would be dedicated to the teaching of a wide variety of professional and generic skills. The eventual outcome of this and similar projects will be important steps in the evolution of Canada's learning continuum and the enhancement of coherence.

### The Need for Change

*Enhancing Coherence*

From the perspective of the learning continuum, how can coherence be established between vocational education and training, on the one hand, and the needs of the labour market, on the other? Are the proper signals being given? Are they being received? Our work shows that there are substantial problems, which can be summarized as follows.

First, the secondary-school system has failed to provide relevant and attractive vocational programs. This comes, at least in part, from communication failures between major segments of the learning community, including employers, teachers, parents, and students. The result is that too many young people are doomed to spend months, if not years, of trial-and-error career search – "dabbling," in effect, in a variety of dead-end jobs.

At the college level, there are promising developments, involving partnerships with business and courses tailored for specific skill needs. But enrolments in science and technology courses do not seem to have paralleled the evolution of those needs. The decrease in enrolments in this area, as a proportion of total enrolments in career courses generally, has only recently begun to level off. In the light of our findings concerning skill shortages, this suggests a lack of timely responsiveness. The rapid growth in the popularity of private career colleges, by contrast, reflects flexibility and placement success.

Next, the apprenticeship system needs a major overhaul with respect to occupational and industrial coverage, coordination of standards, and responsiveness to demand conditions in the labour market. Finally, employer-based training in Canada, widely judged to be inadequate by international standards, is sorely lacking in the small-firm sector – a gap that government programs have so far failed to target successfully.

How might coherence be further enhanced? One promising avenue appears to be improvement in career counselling services. Counsellors themselves complain that in the secondary school of the 1990s, "counselling" covers a bewildering array of topics other than career guidance. Their charges frequently require help or advice about psychological problems associated with drugs, sex, abuse at home, family break-up, as well as academic underachievement. They complain of a lack of useful labour-market information. The academic bias of Canadian secondary schools acts as a deterrent against vocational guidance. Many teachers are not acquainted with the occupational structures of an insurance office, an auto parts factory, or a city hall, and are therefore unaware of the relevant preparation required. Career counselling is not a required course for aspiring teachers. There are no provincial standards or certification, and the function is rarely prominent in ministries of education. This has to be changed.

*Promoting Partnerships*

Partnerships between business and the school system offer one way in which this situation could be substantially improved. They hold out the prospect of direct communication between teachers and employers; for students, they can lead to improved information about the nature of work and employment prospects. The possibilities of mutual benefit are many. Teachers and students gain valuable knowledge about the labour market, while employers assure themselves of adequate supplies of relevant skills enhanced by an exchange of personnel, by "mentoring," by loans or donations of equipment, or by work experience for students through cooperative or apprenticeship programs.

Hundreds of such institutional arrangements are now in place across the country and are being actively promoted by such organizations as the Conference Board of Canada and the Canadian Chamber of Commerce, among others. One illustration of such an arrangement is the Ottawa-Carleton Learning Foundation, in which the participants include five boards of education, over 100 local businesses (including giants like Bell Canada, Bell Northern Research, and Petro Canada), local research institutes and postsecondary institutions, and the relevant provincial ministries. The Foundation administers the Career/Work Education Project, which gives students vocational guidance and work experience, supplies teachers with information about industry, and orients school programs to the skill requirements of employers.

*Developing Cooperative Programs*

One particular form of business/education partnership that has attracted a lot of attention is the so-called cooperative program, in which students alternate periods of study and related work experience, and in which the latter may, in some cases, constitute a credit towards ultimate certification.

The past decade has witnessed very rapid growth in cooperative education at the postsecondary level in Canada. At last count, 35 universities and 48 colleges were offering such programs to over 40,000 students in a vast array of disciplines. Canada has more co-op students per capita than any country in the world; indeed, the University of Waterloo, with 10,000 students in such programs, is the largest postsecondary co-op institution in the world.

Enrolments have burgeoned similarly at the secondary level, and there are now close to 100,000 secondary-school students in government-funded programs. This number is still relatively small, but it is expected to rise, as the federal government recently committed $20 million over the next four years to help develop programs at 114 institutions in Canada, with a particular emphasis on the secondary level.

There are, of course, both pros and cons to such programs. Formal evaluations are few, but observers contend that, at the secondary-school level, co-op programs provide greater relevance and motivation, while reducing absenteeism and drop-out rates. Students gain valuable work experience, and employers gain motivated short-term help on particular assignments and have a chance to screen good candidates for possible permanent employment in the future.

For postsecondary co-op students, additional benefits include the chance to offset a part of their costs and a significant edge in employability over their non-co-op colleagues. The main drawbacks to the students seem to be the limited course selection and curtailment of the "whole campus" experience.

# The Teaching Profession

Teachers are the backbone of the education system, bearing the responsibility for transmitting to children and young adults the knowledge, the skills, and – to a large extent – the values identified by society as being most important for them once they leave school. Teaching also merits attention by virtue of its sheer size as an occupational group. Education is a big industry in Canada: in 1990-91, full-time teachers numbered 293,000 at the elementary and secondary levels, and 62,500 at the postsecondary level.

While it was never a simple task, teaching today faces many new challenges. The economic and social environment is being transformed by the knowledge explosion and by the dizzying pace of technological change, as well as by globalization, growing competitive pressures, and changing social structures. The classroom and its occupants are also being transformed in the process. In big-city schools, one may hear a dozen mother tongues other than English or French. Many students are hungry; many come from broken homes; teachers are increasingly being called upon to fill a vacuum left by institutions that used to be the cornerstones of society, such as the family and the church. Mentally and physically handicapped children have been integrated into the regular public-school system. In many cities, violence in the schools has grown, even in what are considered to be affluent neighbourhoods.

These and other changes are having a profound impact on the socio-economic environment within which education takes place and on the nature of the school-age population. Compounding these problems is the fact that school no longer has the attraction it once had, when education was the recognized path to social promotion.

Often, teachers are ill prepared to meet these challenges. In addition, they must swing with sometimes vast changes in educational philosophies and methodologies, only to find later that the pendulum has begun to move back towards the original position. Yet, given the day-to-day contact that teachers have with students, it is only through their understanding, cooperation, and ability that the education of children and young people takes place.

## *A Profile of Teachers in Canada*

Teachers are getting older! In 1972-73, 44 per cent of elementary- and secondary-school teachers were less than 30 years old (Table 5). By 1989-90, that proportion had dropped to 11 per cent, while that of teachers aged 30-49 had risen from 43 to 73 per cent. This changing age profile reflects the fact that, perhaps more than for any other occupational group, the timing and magnitude of additions to the teaching force are determined by the changing demographic structure of the Canadian population. Sharp increases in the demand for teachers during the late 1960s and early 1970s reflected dramatic growth in the number of schoolchildren as a result of the postwar baby boom. When enrolments later declined following the "baby bust," adjustments to the demand for teachers took the form of sharply reduced rates of hiring.

What has changed very little is the male/female composition of the teaching force. Close to three quarters of elementary-school teachers in 1985-86 were women, but this was true of only one third of teachers at the secondary level. In 1980-81, fewer than one in five school administrators in Canada were women; by 1989-90, the proportion had risen to about one in four. At each successive administrative level – from department head to vice-principal to principal – the proportion of women decreases markedly. Looked at another way, while 25 per cent of male educators in the schools in 1989-90 filled administrative positions, only 6 per cent of female educators did. The scarcity of women at the secondary level, particularly in scientific and technical fields, and their underrepresentation in managerial positions provide few role models for girls and young women to follow.

How good are Canadian teachers? The evidence on this is fragmentary. Certainly, the proportion of teachers holding a university degree has increased dramatically, rising from 40 per cent in 1968-69 to well over 80 per cent by the late 1980s. And paralleling the rising average age of teachers has been an increase in their average number of

**Table 5**

**Age distribution of full-time teachers in elementary and secondary public schools, Canada, 1972-73 and 1989-90**

|  | 1972-73 | 1989-90 |
|---|---|---|
|  | (Per cent) | |
| Less than 30 years old | 44 | 11 |
| 30 to 49 years old | 43 | 73 |
| 50 years old and over | 13 | 16 |
| Total | 100 | 100 |

SOURCE  Based on data from Statistics Canada.

years of experience, which reached close to 15 years by the late 1980s.

Other evidence suggests that large fluctuations in the demand for, and supply of, teachers have an important bearing on the nature of new teaching recruits. Throughout the 1960s, the demand for teachers was very high – so high, in fact, that according to a Statistics Canada study of 1969 university graduates, by 1971 fully half of those who were employed held jobs in the education industry; similarly, 42 per cent of graduates with a bachelor's degree had become teachers. These proportions had decreased by 1978 but nevertheless remained significant: 41 per cent of 1976 university graduates were employed in the education industry, and 37 per cent of those with a bachelor's degree had become teachers. For many of those new recruits, teaching became the alternative when they could not find jobs in other occupations in a labour market that had become saturated with graduates of postsecondary institutions. A study of Ontario teachers [Rees et al.] found, for example, that teaching was reported as the first choice of occupation for about two thirds of both male and female elementary-school teachers, 56 per cent of female secondary-school teachers, and just 37 per cent of male secondary-school teachers, who account for about two thirds of all teaching positions at the secondary level.

All across North America, declining enrolments in the 1970s and well into the 1980s led to a smaller number of teachers being required each year, resulting in an oversupply of newly trained teachers. In the United States, teachers' earnings declined and the quality of new entrants into the profession deteriorated seriously, but the response in Canada was quite different. Teachers' earnings remained high, especially at the lower end of the earnings distribution. That reflected the view that higher earnings would attract higher-quality applicants to teacher-training institutions. Also, the teachers' unions showed considerable strength at the bargaining table.

Interest in the pursuit of teaching as a career has been high in Canada in recent years. Studies from Ontario, British Columbia, and the Atlantic provinces, for example, show that because the number of applicants for teacher-training programs has remained high, faculties of education have been able to choose those with high academic achievement. It would appear, then, that contrary to the U.S. experience, a decrease in the demand for teachers in Canada in the 1980s, combined with strong salary performance, resulted in increased competition for teaching positions, with consequent positive impacts on the academic quality of new entrants. However, because newly trained teachers represented a very small proportion of the total number of teachers, renewal of the teaching force took place only slowly.

*Teacher Demand and Supply*

The labour market for teachers is entering a new phase of growth in demand. Enrolments are beginning to increase; at the same time, over the course of the coming decade a growing number of teachers hired during the expansion of the 1960s will reach retirement age. Concerns are being expressed about the adequacy of teacher supply. The evidence to date, however, is that many more people are interested in acquiring teacher training than there are places in faculties of education. So the *potential* supply is there, but a bottleneck may exist in the capacity of faculties of education to produce new graduates.

Moreover, such overall estimates of teacher demand and supply mask serious shortages that existed even throughout the recent period of teacher oversupply. Those shortages have both a locational and a subject-content aspect.

Remote communities have always faced difficulties in attracting and retaining sufficient numbers of teachers with the right mix of training. But shortages also are becoming apparent in some inner-city locations in the largest metropolitan areas, where high housing costs and sometimes difficult school environments may act as disincentives.

A more general concern is that of shortages of teachers in some subject areas, notably mathematics, the sciences, and technical fields – and in all disciplines in French-language school boards outside Quebec. Often, this results in out-of-field teaching (the teaching of subjects in which the teacher has had little or no training). Often, too, a lack of technical teachers results in secondary schools closing shop facilities.

Shortages of teachers of mathematics, the sciences, and technical subjects are part of a complex web of trends that are affecting most developed countries. The pressures to introduce new technology in order to meet the demands of global competition continue. That requires a technologically and scientifically literate population from which to draw managers and workers alike. A technologically literate population is also needed to provide a good market base that is quick to consume new products and able to make responsible decisions regarding the direction of technological change. Thus growing demands are likely to be placed on the education system to provide children and young people with the knowledge and skills needed to support an economy and society readily adaptable to scientific and technological change. Yet the number of students enrolling in mathematics, science, and engineering at the postsecondary level has been stagnant. That, of course, reduces the size of the pool from which teachers in those fields can be drawn for elementary and secondary schools.

This raises an important aspect of our "coherence" theme – the question of signals. Is the quality of the scientific and technological education offered to students sufficiently high to attract their interest? Why are girls, in particular, not attracted to these fields? Though some gains have been made in the percentage of women enrolled in mathematics, science, and engineering programs at the postsecondary level, the overall female share remains very low. And male postsecondary enrolment in these fields was stagnant during the 1980s. Furthermore, many of those who do actually graduate with science and engineering degrees do not work in those fields after graduation. As the Science Council has argued, this phenomenon occurs because Canadian industry is unable to absorb the skills that these people bring to the labour market, with the consequence that the long-run attractiveness of scientific and technical occupations in Canada is low. On the other hand, occupations in law, medicine, and accounting, for example, offer greater potential returns to individuals in the long run; as a result, more people are being attracted to these occupations.

Clearly, a host of policy issues are associated with the demand and supply of teachers. And while there is no overall shortage of people interested in teaching as a career, there is serious concern about the capacity of the faculties of education not only to provide the needed number of teachers, but also to provide teachers with the right skills and subject specialties.

## Teacher Training

Teacher training, which is of vital importance to the education system, raises many issues. These include initial teacher training, the integration of new teachers into the classroom, and the professional enrichment of experienced teachers.

Recent U.S. reports call for a massive overhaul of the education system, beginning with pre-service and in-service teacher training. Similar views are being voiced in Canada, most recently by the Human Resource Development Committee of the National Advisory Board on Science and Technology. These groups stress that the earning of a teaching degree cannot be a one-shot deal that provides all the knowledge teachers will need throughout their careers; instead, training must be on-going and carefully shaped to meet the changing needs of society and of the teacher. Canadian teachers already take part in in-service training; many of them take courses to gain additional qualifications. Yet research shows that too many of these courses are superficial. Also, school boards often fail to provide their teaching staff with programs for upgrading their professional skills. Teachers' collective agreements provide for several days per year of "professional development," but those days are spread throughout the year and cannot offer teachers in-depth training. As a result, faculties of education face considerable pressures. Not only *new* teachers require special skills to meet present and future demands, but so, too, do those who have been teaching for some years. The constant struggle to keep up with new technologies, changing social and economic needs, growth in knowledge in many fields, and shortages in specific areas all mean that in-service training can be expected to assume growing importance in coming years.

## Teachers' Earnings

A comparison of the earnings of Canadian teachers with those of their peers in other advanced countries is one indication of whether the Canadian system can attract and hold competent teachers. It is widely believed that higher remuneration will attract higher-quality people into teaching and that higher earnings imply higher status in a society (though neither relationship is always directly correlated).

An instructive comparative study of teachers' salaries in a number of advanced countries was completed in the United States in 1988 [see Barro and Suter]. While the wide variety of teaching conditions found in different countries could not be taken into account, care was taken to standardize earnings internationally and to develop a range of indicators. The results show that the average salaries of Canadian teachers during the first half of the 1980s were substantially higher than those of their U.S. counterparts, and higher still than those of teachers in Japan, South Korea, and West Germany (Table 6).

Another indicator considers teachers' salaries relative to gross domestic product (GDP) per capita as a measure of economic status and of the relative economic attractiveness of teaching. On this score, Canadian teachers again outperformed teachers in the United States by a wide margin. However, several other countries – notably South Korea – also performed strongly. On the whole, therefore, Canadian teachers are among the highest-paid in the world and occupy comparatively high positions on the economic ladder.

How well do teachers' earnings compare to those of other occupations in Canada? To answer this question, we used occupations with education and training requirements that are similar to those of the teaching profession. Care was taken to include occupations that, in the past, have offered reasonable alternatives to teaching, such as doctors, lawyers,

**Table 6**

**Average teacher salaries, selected countries, 1980-84**

|   | School type | Year | Salaries[1] | Relative salary[2] |
|---|---|---|---|---|
|   |   |   | (U.S.-dollar equivalents) | (U.S. = 1) |
| Canada | Elementary | 1981 | 21,470 | 1.25 |
|   |   | 1984 | 28,364 | 1.32 |
|   | Secondary | 1981 | 24,821 | 1.37 |
|   |   | 1984 | 31,956 | 1.41 |
| Denmark | Primary + Lower secondary | 1982 | 17,709 | 0.94 |
|   | Upper secondary | 1982 | 25,498 | 1.28 |
| Federal Republic of Germany | Primary | 1982 | 19,026 | 1.01 |
|   | Secondary | 1982 | 21,681 | 1.09 |
| Japan | Elementary + Lower secondary | 1981 | 17,362 | 1.01 |
|   |   | 1984 | 20,359 | 0.95 |
|   | Upper secondary | 1981 | 18,580 | 1.03 |
|   |   | 1984 | 22,406 | 0.99 |
| South Korea | Primary | 1984 | 14,947 | 0.70 |
|   | Middle | 1984 | 13,836 | 0.64 |
|   | Senior | 1984 | 14,947 | 0.66 |
| Sweden | Junior | 1980 | 14,829 | 0.95 |
|   |   | 1984 | 15,759 | 0.73 |
|   | Intermediate | 1980 | 15,740 | 1.01 |
|   |   | 1984 | 16,106 | 0.75 |
|   | Upper + Gymnasium | 1980 | 18,761 | 1.14 |
|   |   | 1984 | 18,803 | 0.83 |
| United Kingdom | Primary | 1982 | 15,648 | 0.83 |
|   |   | 1984 | 16,959 | 0.79 |
|   | Secondary | 1982 | 16,377 | 0.83 |
|   |   | 1984 | 17,731 | 0.78 |
| United States | Elementary | 1981 | 17,241 |   |
|   |   | 1984 | 21,452 |   |
|   | Secondary | 1981 | 18,125 |   |
|   |   | 1984 | 22,667 |   |

1 Earnings in national currency converted to equivalents in U.S. dollars, using standard international conversion factors based on "purchasing power parity" (PPP), which measures the relative costs of standard consumer market baskets in different countries and reflects the number of dollars that would be required in the United States to support the levels of consumption of earners in other countries.
2 Calculated by dividing the average salary of teachers in country X (in U.S.-dollar equivalent), by the average salary of teachers in the United States.
SOURCE Based on Barro and Suter.

engineers, nurses, and social workers. The data, provided by Statistics Canada, gave detailed information on occupational earnings near the bottom, at the middle, and near the top of the earnings scale. Each occupation's earnings profile could thus be traced in 1971, 1981, and 1986.

We found that in 1986, for example, secondary-school and community-college teachers compared very well with other occupations near the bottom of the earnings distribution. And while the position of elementary-school and kindergarten teachers was not as strong, their earnings at this lower level were nonetheless higher than those of seven of the 14 occupations being compared.

So, generally speaking, teachers fare relatively well in terms of starting salaries. But a crucial question for the *retention* of good teachers and their continued motivation and commitment is: what are their future prospects?

Some insights into this issue are provided by Table 7, which shows the "earnings potential" for the teaching occupations in 1986 – that is, the percentage increase in earnings from the bottom 10 per cent of earners to the top 10 per cent. The earnings potential gives a sense of what teachers can hope to achieve throughout their careers with respect to earnings. Secondary-school and college teachers had the smallest earnings potential in 1986. The Canadian average for secondary-school teachers, for example, was 179 per cent; in other words, on average, teachers in the top category earned roughly 79 per cent more than teachers near the bottom of the earnings distribution.

When the earnings potential of the teaching occupations is compared with that of other occupational groups, it is found that while elementary-school teachers rank near the middle, secondary-school teachers in 1986 ranked last in each province.

What conclusions can we draw from this analysis? First, as a group, teachers are relatively well paid, *on average*. Second, teachers appear to do very well, compared with other occupational groups, in terms of starting salaries. Third, however, secondary-school and college teachers face relatively weak career/earnings prospects, even though this is an important incentive for strong performance on the job.

## Career Structure

What the occupational-earnings analysis suggests is that teachers, notably at the secondary-school and college levels, face flat career profiles. While they enjoy the benefits of comparatively high earnings levels early in their careers, the increases they can expect over the course of those careers are low in comparative terms. There are undoubtedly many nonpecuniary reasons why people choose careers in teaching and stay in it. But the common wisdom underlying rising pay structures as an individual progresses through a career would suggest that higher salaries later on in one's career would act as a means of recognizing ability, effort, and experience, and also as an incentive for continued strong performance. One might expect, therefore, that more steeply rising earnings curves would have a stronger impact on motivation and job satisfaction.

The individual teacher is placed within two large bureaucracies: the large administrative systems of school boards and provincial ministries of education; and the network of teachers' unions. Both bureaucracies have worked to ensure that all teachers are treated alike, regardless of their performance. In this, the education bureaucracy has been motivated by the need to provide more or less standardized education programs to millions of schoolchildren. It has sought to do this by standardizing procedures, including the treatment of teachers. Teachers' unions, on the other hand,

### Table 7
**Earnings potential[1] in selected teaching occupations, Canada and provinces, 1986**

|  | Teachers |  |  | Administrators (teaching and related) |
|---|---|---|---|---|
|  | Community college/CÉGEP | Secondary school | Elementary and kindergarten |  |
| Newfoundland | 192 | 162 | 165 | 192 |
| Prince Edward Island | -- | 159 | 187 | 221 |
| Nova Scotia | 188 | 171 | 216 | 238 |
| New Brunswick | 162 | 160 | 187 | 196 |
| Quebec | 165 | 162 | 219 | 206 |
| Ontario | 232 | 179 | 269 | 250 |
| Manitoba | 173 | 163 | 221 | 238 |
| Saskatchewan | 277 | 171 | 201 | 215 |
| Alberta | 197 | 172 | 227 | 240 |
| British Columbia | 212 | 161 | 243 | 246 |
| **Canada** | **190** | **179** | **242** | **236** |

1 Earnings potential is calculated as: $\dfrac{\text{lower dollar limit of top 10 per cent of earners}}{\text{upper dollar limit of bottom 10 per cent of earners}} \times 100$.

SOURCE  Estimates by the Economic Council, based on data from Employment and Immigration Canada.

in pursuing fair and equitable treatment of their members have, in the end, ensured that all teachers are treated equally.

The outcome is that promotion within the teaching ranks generally occurs in lock-step fashion, with annual increases dependent on educational background and years of experience. Teachers can return to school to earn more-advanced degrees as a means of progressing to a higher earnings category, or they may transfer into the administrative ranks. Otherwise, personal initiative and motivation do not come to bear on earnings to any significant extent. Teaching has been referred to as a "strangely 'careerless' career." Beginning teachers' salaries are high, compared with those of more experienced teachers, and little distinction is made between good teachers and poor ones.

Earlier, we pointed out the positive role that could be played by building up a school ethos. The leadership of school principals is clearly fundamental in developing an achievement-oriented ethos. But to be successful the principal needs the enthusiastic commitment of highly trained, capable, and dedicated teachers, less bound by the constraints of bureaucracy and with greater opportunity to build upon the strengths of the most able teachers. Thus principals need the freedom to select a group of teachers that is best able to work together as a team.

*Summary*

In looking at the education system and at the place of teachers in it, we are faced with a seeming paradox. Today's teachers are highly educated and well paid, have several years' experience, and have seen the pupil/teacher ratio drop substantially in recent years. Yet there has not been any significant improvement in student achievement. On the contrary, we conclude that the performance of the education system in Canada is just not good enough to assure Canadians of an improving standard of living in coming decades.

Identifying the role of teachers in this lacklustre performance on the basis of highly aggregated descriptive statistics is very difficult. The acquisition of a university degree is no guarantee that the individual can teach; age and experience can improve the performance of some individuals but lead to disillusionment and "burn-out" in others; and shrinking pupil/teacher ratios tell us little about the changing character of students in the classroom and the problems that teachers face. It would be dishonest – or at the very least misleading – to state that all, or even most, teachers in Canada are either good or bad. All of us, whether former or current students, parents, or simple observers of the education scene, know that the school system is made up of both good and bad teachers. They cannot be identified by their looks or their degrees, but only by their performance in the classroom. Students and their parents usually know who they are. It would be surprising if principals did not also know. But the bureaucracy, including the unions, has been very successful in protecting the jobs of teachers who are just not good enough. At the same time, excellent teachers have not been sufficiently rewarded.

What can be done to help the teaching profession contribute to an improved education system in Canada? A useful first step is to screen teachers-in-training more carefully. Conventional training methods give novice teachers too little classroom exposure. They need more time to discover whether they actually like working with children and young people before they commit themselves to a teaching career. Another useful step is to explicitly recognize that not all teachers are equal in ability and performance. Some teachers are simply better than others, and the system should make more effective use of its best teachers' skills. At the same time, a route out of the classroom must be in place to promote the departure of poor teachers.

## Costs and Financing

There is a widespread perception that Canada's learning system not only produces unsatisfactory results but is also very expensive. The validity of this perception can be tested by examining a number of indicators of cost. How does Canada compare with other countries? How do cost levels and structures vary across the provinces? And, given the current climate of severe fiscal constraint at all levels of government, it is clearly important to understand how the system is funded.

### *Financial Commitment to Education*

#### *International Comparisons*

One indicator of the scale of a country's financial commitment to education is the proportion of GDP allocated to that sector. Data from the OECD show that in 1989, for example, public-sector spending on education in Canada amounted to 6.2 per cent of GDP, placing this country in fifth position, behind the Scandinavian countries and the Netherlands, but ahead of the United States, the United Kingdom, France, West Germany, and Japan (Table 8).

The share of educational spending accounted for by the private sector is proportionately very small in most OECD

**Table 8**

**Indicators of public-sector spending on education relative to gross domestic product, selected OECD countries, 1989**

|  | Spending on education/GDP ||  Proportion of the population enrolled in education*** | Public-sector spending per student/ GDP per capita ||
| --- | --- | --- | --- | --- | --- |
|  | Public sector | Private sources |  |  |  |
|  | (Per cent) |||| (Rank) |
| Norway | 7.2 | 0.2 | 22.9 | 31.4 | 3 |
| Sweden | 7.1 | – | 16.8 | 42.3 | 1 |
| Denmark | 7.0 | 0.3 | 20.6 | 34.0 | 2 |
| Netherlands | 6.5* | 0.3* | 22.9 | 28.4 | 4 |
| **Canada** | **6.2** | **0.6** | **24.5** | **25.3** | **7** |
| New Zealand | 5.6* | – | 27.1 | 20.6 | 13 |
| Austria | 5.5 | – | 20.3 | 27.1 | 5 |
| France | 5.3 | 1.0 | 25.6 | 20.7 | 12 |
| Australia | 5.3*** | 0.4*** | 22.3 | 23.8 | 9 |
| United Kingdom | 5.0** | – | 24.3 | 20.5 | 14 |
| Switzerland | 5.0 | – | 19.7 | 25.4 | 6 |
| Italy | 5.0*** | – | 20.1 | 24.9 | 8 |
| Belgium | 4.9* | – | 23.5 | 20.9 | 11 |
| United States | 4.8*** | 1.7*** | 24.9 | 19.3 | 16 |
| Japan | 4.7* | 1.4* | 22.0 | 21.4 | 10 |
| West Germany | 4.1* | 0.2* | 20.6 | 19.9 | 15 |

*1988.
**1987.
***1986.
SOURCE Estimates by the Economic Council, based on data from the OECD.

member countries, though some international differences are apparent. In the late 1980s, for example, this type of spending as a proportion of GDP amounted to 0.6 per cent in Canada, 1.7 per cent in the United States, and 0.2 per cent in West Germany. When these additional expenditures are taken into account, Canadian spending on education as a proportion of GDP still exceeds that of the United States, Japan, and France, though the gap is significantly narrowed.

The relative magnitude of a country's spending on education will be influenced by the relative size of its student population, which in turn depends partly on the age structure. Countries with a high rate of participation in education can be expected to allocate a relatively higher proportion of GDP to the education sector. The Canadian rate of participation in education is high by international standards. As shown in Table 8, 24 per cent of the Canadian population was enrolled in formal education in 1986, placing Canada in the leading group of countries, which also included New Zealand, the United Kingdom, the United States, and France.

A particularly useful measure of a country's financial commitment to education, adjusted for the relative size of the student population, is the ratio of education expenditures per student to GDP per capita – in other words, spending per student relative to total income per person. Using this indicator, we find that Canada ranked seventh out of a total of 16 OECD countries in 1989; the United States had the lowest ratio among this group. The high-spending countries were Sweden, Denmark, Norway, and the Netherlands. West Germany and Japan ranked in the bottom half of the list, their relative per-student spending being slightly lower than Canada's. These findings are disturbing, since Germany and Japan appear to be more successful in terms of the overall performance of the education system.

Canadian spending in education is not remarkably different from that of other OECD countries. In some respects, this result is somewhat surprising, as there are features of the Canadian education system that can significantly affect costs. One obvious characteristic that distinguishes Canada is its large size and the low population density found in many regions. Another is the proliferation of school systems and school boards in many provinces, reflecting constitutional provisions designed to protect religious and linguistic rights.

There is ample evidence to suggest that reductions in total costs could be achieved by restructuring and rationalizing school boards within provinces. Data from provincial governments and individual school boards clearly show that the cost per student has an inverse relationship with the number of students – in larger school boards, costs per student are lower. Reducing the number of school boards in a given jurisdiction thus appears to be cost-effective. The New Brunswick experience, in which the total number of school boards is to be reduced from 42 to 15, is a good example of the kind of rationalization that is possible. Naturally, care must be taken to ensure that the new, rationalized system will remain capable of meeting the various special needs of a very diverse population.

A further distinguishing feature of the Canadian education system is the multiplicity of cultural backgrounds found among its student population. In 1986, 16 per cent of Canadian residents were born in other countries – one of the highest proportions among OECD countries. This rich linguistic and cultural diversity naturally poses special problems for educators. Facing up to these challenges entails costs that are obviously not incurred by less heterogeneous societies.

*Spending by the Provinces*

Expenditures in Canada's public school systems have climbed over the past 30 years. For example, spending per student (in 1981 dollars) at the elementary and secondary levels rose from about $1,100 in 1961 to $3,660 in 1989. The major determinants of per-student costs are the wage bill and the pupil/teacher ratio. It has been estimated that during the period 1961-89, teachers' real wages grew by 3.7 per cent per year, on average – about the same rate as that of real wages in the entire economy. This increase in real wages is estimated to have contributed about half of the rise in real spending per student. In addition, the pupil/teacher ratio fell dramatically – from 26 to 1 in 1960-61 to 16 to 1 in 1989-90. The impact of such a large decrease in the ratio is important: more than a fourth of the total increase in real spending per student can be attributed to it.

Current expenditures on education (in 1989-90) are shown for each of the provinces in Figure 12. There is considerable provincial variation in the share of expenditures allocated to each level in the system. Ontario, for example, which accounted for over one third of total Canadian expenditures on education in 1989-90, allocated the largest share of its spending to the elementary and secondary levels; postsecondary vocational training received the smallest share. By contrast, the provinces with the largest share of provincial spending going to vocational training were those in the Atlantic region. To a certain extent, these differences in spending patterns reflect variations in the structure of provincial education systems. This is particularly true for Quebec, where the secondary level ends with Grade 11. Beyond that level, students attend CÉGEPs, which are part of the college sector and are allocated a substantial portion of spending on both vocational and pre-university training. The provinces engage in some vocational training at the secondary level, but it is relatively small.

Variation across the provinces is also evident in figures on spending per student. In 1989-90, average expenditures per student were highest in Manitoba, Ontario, Alberta, and Quebec – and lowest in the Atlantic provinces (Table 9). Because of its size, spending at the elementary/secondary level determines the provinces' relative positions. Indeed, spending per elementary/secondary student averaged $4,800 in the Atlantic provinces and $6,000 in Quebec and Ontario.

**Figure 12**

**Total expenditures on education, by school level and by province, Canada, 1989-90**

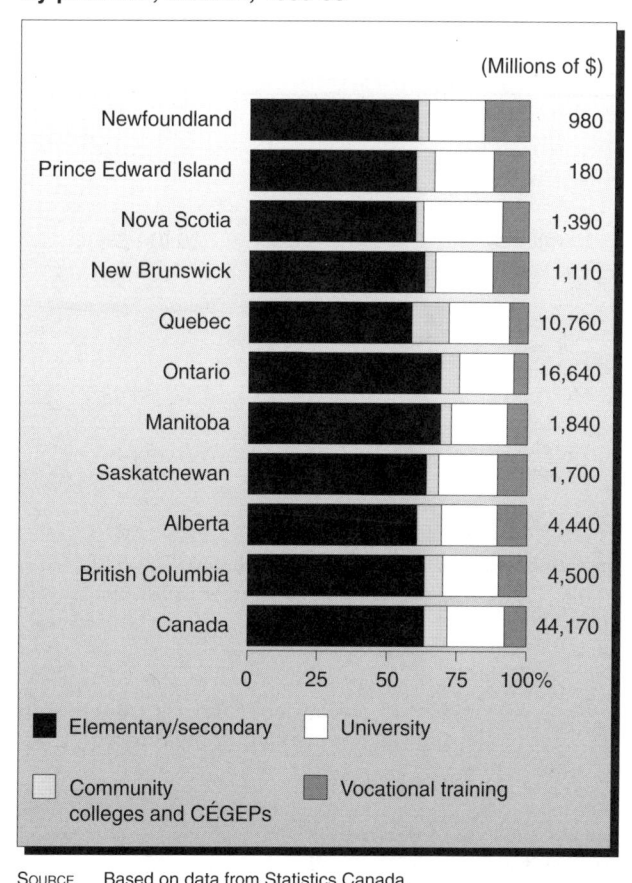

| Province | (Millions of $) |
|---|---|
| Newfoundland | 980 |
| Prince Edward Island | 180 |
| Nova Scotia | 1,390 |
| New Brunswick | 1,110 |
| Quebec | 10,760 |
| Ontario | 16,640 |
| Manitoba | 1,840 |
| Saskatchewan | 1,700 |
| Alberta | 4,440 |
| British Columbia | 4,500 |
| Canada | 44,170 |

Legend: Elementary/secondary, University, Community colleges and CÉGEPs, Vocational training

SOURCE Based on data from Statistics Canada.

### Table 9
**Total expenditures per student,[1] by school level and by province, Canada, 1989-90**

|  | Elementary/secondary | College/CÉGEP | University | All levels (weighted average) |
|---|---|---|---|---|
|  | (Dollars) | | | |
| Newfoundland | 4,660 | 10,910 | 15,130 | 5,760 |
| Prince Edward Island | 4,270 | 12,310 | 14,790 | 5,490 |
| Nova Scotia | 5,080 | 14,020 | 14,050 | 6,500 |
| New Brunswick | 5,100 | 16,210 | 13,130 | 6,190 |
| Quebec | 5,740 | 8,100 | 14,990 | 7,040 |
| Ontario | 6,170 | 9,560 | 13,530 | 7,140 |
| Manitoba | 6,050 | 17,090 | 15,130 | 7,170 |
| Saskatchewan | 5,320 | 23,970 | 15,050 | 6,580 |
| Alberta | 5,670 | 14,080 | 16,600 | 7,140 |
| British Columbia | 5,330 | 8,470 | 19,360 | 6,550 |
| **Canada[2]** | **5,790** | **9,540** | **15,010** | **6,980** |

1 Full-time-equivalent student.
2 Including the Yukon and Northwest Territories.
SOURCE Estimates by the Economic Council, based on data from Statistics Canada.

### Table 10
**Total expenditures per student as a proportion of GDP per capita, by school level and by province, Canada, 1989-90**

|  | Elementary/secondary | College/CÉGEP | University | All levels (weighted average) |
|---|---|---|---|---|
|  | (Per cent) | | | |
| Newfoundland | 31.5 | 73.9 | 102.4 | 39.0 |
| Prince Edward Island | 29.8 | 85.8 | 103.8 | 38.3 |
| Nova Scotia | 28.2 | 77.8 | 77.9 | 36.1 |
| New Brunswick | 29.2 | 92.8 | 75.2 | 35.4 |
| Quebec | 25.0 | 35.3 | 65.3 | 30.7 |
| Ontario | 21.9 | 33.9 | 48.0 | 25.3 |
| Manitoba | 28.5 | 80.5 | 71.3 | 33.8 |
| Saskatchewan | 26.7 | 120.5 | 75.7 | 33.1 |
| Alberta | 20.3 | 50.5 | 59.6 | 25.6 |
| British Columbia | 21.7 | 34.5 | 78.8 | 26.7 |
| **Canada** | **23.3** | **38.4** | **60.5** | **28.1** |

SOURCE Estimates by the Economic Council, based on data from Statistics Canada.

This regional spending pattern plays a significant role in explaining the poorer educational achievement of the Atlantic provinces.

As in the case of the international comparisons discussed earlier, it is useful to relate provincial per-student spending levels to provincial GDP per capita (Table 10). The highest ratio across all school levels in 1989-90 was to be found in the Atlantic provinces, largely because per-capita GDP in those provinces is relatively low, so that even low levels of per-student expenditure result in a relatively high financial burden on their residents. The weak performance of Atlantic students in mathematics, science, and literacy tests (see above) is particularly worrisome, given the greater

**Table 11**

**School-board expenditures, by component and by province, Canada, 1986-87**

| | Teachers' salaries | Instructional supplies | Administration[1] | Conveyance | Plant operation | Capital expenditures | Others |
|---|---|---|---|---|---|---|---|
| | | | | (Per cent) | | | |
| Newfoundland | 69.1 | 1.5 | 6.1 | 5.2 | 9.1 | 8.0 | 1.0 |
| Prince Edward Island | 61.1 | 0.9 | 6.3 | 8.4 | 10.5 | 12.3 | 0.5 |
| Nova Scotia | 68.0 | 1.3 | 4.6 | 4.9 | 9.9 | 7.6 | 3.7 |
| New Brunswick[2] | 70.3 | 1.5 | 5.5 | 7.9 | 13.1 | 0.7 | 1.0 |
| Quebec | 55.8 | 2.1 | 8.1 | 6.5 | 9.6 | 8.3 | 9.6 |
| Ontario | 63.4 | 2.8 | 7.5 | 5.2 | 11.7 | 6.2 | 3.2 |
| Manitoba | 56.8 | 3.3 | 8.0 | 4.4 | 10.9 | 11.5 | 5.1 |
| Saskatchewan | 56.9 | 3.8 | 4.6 | 7.6 | 11.4 | 8.4 | 7.3 |
| Alberta | 59.9 | 2.6 | 5.6 | 5.3 | 11.7 | 12.2 | 2.7 |
| British Columbia | 58.5 | 2.4 | 5.0 | 2.5 | 14.1 | 10.5 | 7.0 |
| **Canada** | **60.5** | **2.5** | **7.0** | **5.4** | **11.2** | **8.1** | **5.3** |

1 Statistics Canada's definition of administration is used here. Some of the differences in the structure of provincial education systems are not captured by the use of a single definition, however. This factor explains Quebec's high share, in particular.
2 In New Brunswick, most capital expenditures fall under the responsibility of the Department of Education rather than of the school boards.
SOURCE  Estimates by the Economic Council, based on data from Statistics Canada.

relative financial burden borne by the provinces in the region.

The two provinces with the lowest per-student spending/per-capita GDP, averaged across all school levels, were Ontario and Alberta. The burden of providing education in these provinces is thus relatively light, overall, though we should note that fiscal capacity varies significantly across school boards within provinces.

With respect to the composition of spending on education, our analysis shows that interprovincial differences in relative spending levels reflect different spending patterns. Table 11 shows that the share of teachers' salaries in total school-board costs for elementary and secondary schools, averaged across all provinces, was about 60 per cent in 1986-87. This proportion was very high in the Atlantic provinces (averaging 67 per cent) and very low in Quebec (56 per cent), reflecting very low increases in teachers' salaries in that province during the 1980s. While salaries in Quebec and Ontario rose at an average annual rate of 12.6 and 10.7 per cent, respectively, between 1976-77 and 1981-82, the corresponding figures were 4.0 and 6.6 per cent between 1981-82 and 1988-89. By contrast, the growth in per-capita personal income across Canada grew at average annual rates of 11.9 and 7.2 per cent over those two periods.

Capital expenditures constitute about 8 per cent of total school-board costs. Again, interprovincial differences are quite striking: Ontario spends the smallest share on capital formation, while the western provinces spend the highest share, with the majority of them devoting more than 10 per cent to investment. (In New Brunswick, capital expenses are not counted among school-board costs.)

The shares of administration in total school-board expenses are also interesting. Historical data shows that this particular component has grown at a very rapid rate – from less than 3 per cent of total costs in 1961 to close to 7 per cent in the late 1980s. Currently, Quebec and Manitoba spend the highest share for administration – about 8 per cent of the total and Ontario ranks third at 7.5 per cent. In contrast, the other three western provinces all have very low administration costs. Some of the differences between provinces can be explained by differences in the definition of administrative costs. In some provinces, for example, school boards report the salaries of the principal and vice-principals in the administrative category, while in others they are reported among the teachers' category. But even when these differences are taken into account, Quebec still spends a greater proportion on administration.

These numbers show only the cost of administering school boards. However, as can be seen in Table 12, even when we add the costs of maintaining the various provincial education departments, the picture is not radically changed. Quebec's spending per student remains ahead of the other provinces, and British Columbia and Saskatchewan remain near the bottom of the ranking in this respect. Part of the reason for that spending pattern lies in the fact that Quebec's ministry of education plays a more prominent role in the education system than do its counterparts in other provinces. For example, the Quebec ministry funds one of the highest shares of school-board expenses. In addition, it acts as the employer in centralized, province-wide collective bargaining with the teachers' unions. The broader range of roles and responsibilities that it assumes contributes to a higher level of costs than in other provinces. Also, in some provinces some of the research in education is being done in nongovernmental institutions, while elsewhere (particularly in Quebec) all of the work is centralized within the provincial government.

Differences in the cost structure of school boards can also provide a partial explanation for provincial spending differences. Table 13 shows spending for three types of school boards in each of four different provinces – Nova Scotia, Quebec, Saskatchewan, and British Columbia.

**Table 12**

**Spending per student on administration,[1] Canada, by province, 1986**

| | School boards | School boards and education departments |
|---|---|---|
| | (Dollars per student) | |
| Newfoundland | 191 | 237 |
| Prince Edward Island | 212 | 233 |
| Nova Scotia | 166 | 191 |
| New Brunswick | 161 | 179 |
| Quebec | 398 | 440 |
| Ontario | 336 | 359 |
| Manitoba | 356 | 384 |
| Saskatchewan | 184 | 232 |
| Alberta | 257 | 284 |
| British Columbia | 194 | 215 |
| **Canada** | **304** | **334** |

[1] Statistics Canada's definition of administration is used here. Some of the differences in the structure of provincial education systems are not captured by the use of a single definition, however. This factor explains Quebec's high share, in particular.

SOURCE Estimates by the Economic Council, based on data from Statistics Canada.

**Table 13**

**School-board expenditures per student, rural and urban regions in four provinces, Canada, 1987-90**

|  | Nova Scotia (1989-90) | | Quebec (1987-88) | | Saskatchewan (1988-89) | | British Columbia (1989-90) | |
| --- | --- | --- | --- | --- | --- | --- | --- | --- |
|  | Total | Excluding transportation | Total | Excluding transportation | Total | Excluding transportation | Total | Excluding transportation |
|  | (Dollars per student) | | | | | | | |
| Urban regions | 4,663 | 4,597 | 4,629 | 4,243 | 3,968 | 3,897 | 4,210 | 4,160 |
| Semi-urban regions | 3,783 | 3,616 | 4,845 | 4,319 | 4,257 | 4,014 | – | – |
| Rural regions | 4,180 | 3,803 | 5,223 | 4,697 | 4,663 | 4,070 | 5,242 | 4,819 |

SOURCE  Estimates by the Economic Council, based on data from various provincial documents.

Representative school boards were chosen from each of three types: urban, semi-urban, and rural. The results show that, in general, the lower the degree of urbanization, the higher the total expenditure per student. This pattern may be caused by several factors. The first, and most obvious, is the difference in population density, leading to higher transportation costs for rural school boards. But as Table 13 also shows, higher costs per student in rural boards remain even when transportation costs are excluded. Teachers' salaries – an important component of per-student costs – displayed the same rural/urban pattern in the provinces for which we had data, possibly reflecting rural/urban differences in average teachers' salaries and pupil/teacher ratios. Economies of scale may be another factor: urban boards, which generally tend to have more students, have a lower cost per student.

*The Financing of Education*

The context within which the current debate on education and training is taking place is one of severely constrained fiscal capacity. For that reason alone, a brief review of funding sources is appropriate. Furthermore, the increasingly evident need to improve the performance of the system underscores the importance of developing funding approaches with a strict accountability orientation. More specifically, the discussion of costs revealed that although the poorer provinces spend less per student in absolute terms, their taxpayers nevertheless face a higher relative burden than their counterparts in the richer provinces. Here, we suggest that the ability of provinces to raise funds from taxpayers may be crucial in any attempt to increase the performance of the education system.

Until the Second World War and the baby boom that followed, the elementary/secondary system in most provinces was structured into a large number of very small school districts, and the local residential tax base was the major source of funding for education. Rapid growth in enrolment, in the number of teachers, and in teachers' salaries severely strained the local tax bases and led to growing involvement in the system by provincial governments and to consolidation of local school districts into regional boards. For example, in 1971 Quebec consolidated 1,100 local school boards into 63 regional boards.

Today, there are important similarities in the way the provinces finance their respective education systems. In general, provincial funding is provided from a mix of general revenue and specific tax levies, as well as property taxes in some cases, and is delivered to school boards through formulas that take into account general as well as specific needs. These funding arrangements are often referred to as "foundation plans" because of the commitment by the province to ensure a minimum funding base for local education programs (see box).

There are also differences among the various provincial financing systems. An important difference lies in the sources of funding. Some school boards rely heavily on local property taxes as a source of revenue, while others depend on provincial funding. For example, the provincial government's contribution to the funding of education in the Atlantic provinces averages about 92 per cent; in Quebec, it is 90 per cent. Municipal funding plays only a minor role in those provinces. In other provinces, such as Ontario and the western provinces, the municipal share of funding is around a third, with a high of 45 per cent in Ontario.

There is one significant exception to foundation plans, called the "resource-cost" model, which is based on the notion that the provincial government should specify and fund a basic level of education program and that any "extras" should be provided entirely by the local tax base. This approach requires that service levels be precisely defined and that accurate costing of these levels be developed for each school district. Funding is then provided for that

---

**General Model for Provincial Funding Arrangements**

Education finance systems frequently aim to achieve three related forms of equity: horizontal equity seeks to treat similar students alike, regardless of location; vertical equity seeks to ensure that unlike students are treated according to their specific needs; and taxpayer equity seeks to ensure that the burden of providing resources to the system is borne as fairly as possible.

Provincial funding is delivered to school boards through formulas that usually have three main components:

- The basic level of grant is called the *block* or *foundation* grant, which typically is a flat amount per pupil and may vary slightly within a defined range.
- Specific needs are supported through *categorical* grants for services such as transportation, special needs, and language programs.
- Equity with regard to tax capacity is supported through *equalization* grants, which are paid to school boards to enhance their revenue capacity. Sometimes, such grants are based on the equalization of balanced assessment per pupil, so that all school districts have the same per-pupil income from the same tax effort. Alternatively, only a portion of the tax effort is equalized; in other cases, the equalization is less than 100 per cent.

level of service. There is no set foundation level; each district has a unique level based on the actual local costs of delivering the basic level of service standard. The resource-cost model stands in contrast to foundation plans, which – though they may contain fiscal ceilings or caps – do not spell out these limits in operational terms.

Local school districts can still have significant autonomy in a resource-cost environment. The revenue received by the school district is intended to cover the standard costs of delivering education services, as mandated by the province. Local trustees and administrators, however, retain the freedom to decide how the funds are allocated to specific activities – increasing class sizes, for example – in order to free up funds for a special program. Programs specific to a given district can also be supported through local taxes. Because such programs are financed in full by the local tax base, accountability to the local taxpayers is enhanced. However, that may also mean that poorer regions are unable to develop special programs.

Only one province – British Columbia – has implemented a resource-cost model. Introduced in 1983-84, the B.C. approach is still undergoing a process of evolution. The system rests on two fundamental criteria: equity and accountability. Equity is pursued through strong fiscal controls. For example, local school boards are not given access to the rich commercial property tax base; provincially mandated program levels cannot be exceeded without a local referendum; and new services cannot be started without service levels being established by the province. Interestingly, the fiscal framework – an elaborate system of costing and accounting – was put into place first. Accountability is the second cornerstone of the B.C. system. The province has been investing heavily in the development of outcome indicators, and there is hope that discussion of the system will go beyond such concerns as the accuracy of the costing of specific levels of instruction and focus on the definition of appropriate service levels in relation to desired educational *outcomes*.

### Summary

This brief overview of the financing of elementary/secondary education in Canada only hints at the range of funding mechanisms that are in place throughout the country. Despite this variety, no analysis exists of the relationships between the different financing approaches in Canada and, in particular, of their effectiveness in terms of student outcomes. In adopting the resource-cost model, British Columbia is attempting to identify an explicit link between funding levels and education outcomes. The development of the B.C. approach therefore warrants close observation.

Summing up, certain key points should be emphasized. First, the common perception that Canada spends more than almost any country on earth must be modified. Per-student spending as a percentage of GDP is generous but not outstanding, by international standards. Canada spends more than Germany and Japan, but less than many other countries. Second, given the fact that Canada is a high-cost country because of the dispersion of its population over a vast area and of the presence of several layers of linguistic and religious administrations, it is difficult to say how much is too much, as there is no proper benchmark against which to compare the Canadian system. Third, interprovincial differences in the burden of educational costs must be considered a concern, particularly because that burden appears to be heaviest in those less prosperous provinces where student achievement is the lowest. The Atlantic provinces are clearly overstretched in trying to maintain their education systems. On the other hand, even though Ontario's per-student expenditures are among the highest in Canada, they are relatively low in relation to per-capita GDP. Given the province's unsatisfactory performance in education, however, funding decisions warrant close scrutiny. Fourth, there are some striking differences in cost structures among the provinces: for example, Quebec is, in relative terms, a high spender on administration and a low spender on teachers' salaries. Finally, it is clear that current funding formulas in most systems are not linked to educational outcomes. Given current fiscal realities, the accountability features of British Columbia's resource-cost model are very pertinent. It is too soon to say whether this system is "right" for all, but certainly other provinces will want to monitor it closely.

## Education and Training: An International Perspective

In order to assess Canada's relative position among the industrial nations and the possible directions it might take in the future, it is important to determine how its system of education and training differs from those of the most successful countries. Like those of its main trading partners, Canada's economy offers high wages. If Canadians want to maintain their standard of living, the work force must constantly keep abreast of the best practice and best use of technology developed at home and abroad. But Canadians do not set the pace and nature of change: "Improving human resources in other nations sets a rising standard even to maintain current competitive positions" [Porter, p. 628].

The analysis requires that we show how Canada ranks internationally in terms of the characteristics and performance not only of its education system but also of its labour market and its economy. The three systems are closely

40   A Lot to Learn

linked, and all must perform well if Canadians are to achieve on-going gains in living standards. Four major messages can be drawn from our analysis:

– Canada finds itself in the middle of a group of 18 industrialized countries. Its position reflects an unbalanced performance, with some strengths but also with weaknesses that are major deterrents to global success.

– A nation can achieve "more bang for the buck" from its education and training systems if there is coherence with the labour market and with economic performance, as in Germany and Japan, for example.

– In Canada, the lack of such coherence condemns many young people to a haphazard transition from school to work and fails to prepare adult learners for ever-changing skill needs.

– The particular aspects of coherence upon which Canada must concentrate are: the transmission of clear signals by Canadian employers about skill needs and expectations; the effective reception of those signals by the education and training systems; and the active cooperation of social partners in fashioning an appropriate response.

*Canada's International Standing*

*An Uneven Record*

To assess Canada's relative socio-economic performance, relevant indicators in the three areas – education, the labour market, and economic performance – were compared for 18 OECD countries (see box and Table 14). This comparison provides an indication of Canada's relative standing in the quest for productivity and income growth. Canada ranks ninth overall and also occupies a middle position in each of the categories – better than the lowest-ranking countries, but far from the top. It is not that Canada's ranking is so low; after all, three leading industrial countries (the United Kingdom, France, and Italy) rank worse. Rather, it is that the imbalance among the indicators is a clear sign that this country is not living up to its potential. We showed, earlier in this Statement, that resources and opportunities are generally good for the academically oriented child. But for others, signals are unclear; pathways are confused; and rewards are uncertain. Overall, Canada seems to be accepting mediocrity as the norm, when it has the potential to achieve excellence.

The indicators discussed here include educational attainment and opportunities, universality of access, drop-out levels, interest in scientific fields, the strength of vocational education, the degree of flexibility in industry, and the state of industrial relations.

**Table 14**

**Ranking of major OECD countries on three sets of indicators[1]**

| Overall ranking | Country | Education | Labour market | Economy |
|---|---|---|---|---|
| 1 | Japan | 4 | 1 | 1 |
| 2 | West Germany | 1 | 5 | 2 |
| 3 | Switzerland | 7 | 2 | 3 |
| 4 | Austria | 6 | 4 | 4 |
| 5 | United States | 8 | 3 | 7 |
| 6 | Finland | 2 | 10 | 6 |
| 7 | Denmark | 5 | 7 | 14 |
| 8 | Sweden | 3 | 12 | 15 |
| 9 | **Canada** | **11** | **8** | **10** |
| 10 | Norway | 9 | 11 | 9 |
| 11 | Netherlands | 12 | 13 | 5 |
| 12 | United Kingdom | 15 | 6 | 11 |
| 13 | Belgium | 10 | 17 | 8 |
| 14 | Australia | 14 | 14 | 12 |
| 15 | France | 13 | 15 | 13 |
| 16 | New Zealand | 16 | 9 | 16 |
| 17 | Italy | 17 | 16 | 17 |
| 18 | Spain | 18 | 18 | 18 |

1  The education set includes 16 indicators – e.g., enrolment rate at age 17; enrolment rate in higher education; public expenditures in education per capita; an evaluation, by business leaders, of whether in-company training meets the needs of a competitive economy, and so on. The labour set includes 16 indicators – e.g., employment/ population ratio; share of youth unemployment in total unemployment; days lost due to industrial disputes; an evaluation, by business leaders, of the degree of employees' identification with company's objectives, and so on. The economy set includes 15 indicators – e.g., rate of growth; R&D expenditures by business; exports of engineering products; an evaluation, by business leaders, of the government's ability to promote competitiveness, and so on.

SOURCE  Estimates by the Economic Council, based on data from the OECD; *The World Competitiveness Report,* 1990 and 1991; and UNDP's *The Human Development Report,* 1991.

*Strengths . . .*

By international standards, the Canadian population enjoys a high level of educational attainment: with more than 12 years of schooling, on average, Canadians are second only to their American neighbours. Note, however, that the school year in North America is one of the shortest in the world – 180 to 185 days, compared with 243 days in Japan and with between 226 and 240 days in Germany, for example. Thus, over a period of 10 years of compulsory schooling Japanese children spend far more time in school – the equivalent of more than three additional school years – than do North American children. Consequently, if the data were adjusted to reflect differences in the length of the school year – and possibly the actual time spent in the classroom – educational attainment in Canada would more closely resemble that in Japan and Germany.

> **Indicators for Education, Labour Market, and Economy**
>
> In each of the three groups, indicators were selected on the basis of their relevance and their capacity to differentiate among countries. Two main data sources were used: *Education in OECD Countries, 1987-88* (published by the Organisation for Economic Co-operation and Development), and *The World Competitiveness Report* for 1990 and 1991. This latter source provided two types of data: factual observations coming originally, for example, from OECD or UNESCO sources; and data based on an original survey of business leaders in various countries. The participants in the latter were asked to rate the performance of their country of residence in terms of a large number of factors. Such views are important because in the three systems – education, labour market, economy – performance assessment by essential economic actors plays a major role, alongside the "objective" measured elements, in determining behaviour. Some of the results of this survey have been incorporated into our analysis; in the text, they are clearly identified as business leaders' opinions.
>
> The indicators referred to in this section were all used in this analysis. (Details about the indicators and the standardization procedure can be found in the research report associated with this statement.)

Canada and the United States display another positive characteristic in that there are no significant gender differences in educational level, either for the population as a whole or for young people alone. By contrast, in most other countries fewer girls than boys complete secondary school. Access to postsecondary studies – including both universities and community colleges – is also significantly higher in North America than in most other countries and regions. Today, as in the past, North America appears to provide greater assurance of equal opportunity and universal access to the education system.

*... and Weaknesses*

One major concern about the Canadian education system is that close to one third of students do not complete their secondary schooling. A large proportion of secondary-school graduates do go on to university, but many of them also drop out before completing their studies at that level.

Moreover, the scientific fields of study deemed essential to a country's future attract a smaller proportion of students in Canada than in many other countries. While this is especially evident among female students, male enrolments are also relatively low. The relatively low enrolments in scientific disciplines may reflect – and, at the same time, reinforce – Canada's low commitment of resources to research and development.

In Canada, vocational preparation is not treated as a credible alternative to the academic stream in secondary schools. A significant proportion of young people do attend the vocational stream of community colleges or CÉGEPs, but the courses tend to be theoretical, with insufficient hands-on, in-company training experience and certification.

The lack of opportunity for secondary-school students to take appropriate and adequate vocational training need not lead to economic failure. Japan has been very successful in making good this "deficiency," thanks to the involvement of employers in vocational training. This sort of commitment is virtually nonexistent in Canada. Moreover, the Canadian apprenticeship system is limited in coverage and is not responsive to labour-market needs. A major shortcoming of this and other vocational programs is that certification does not confer the instant recognition and widespread acceptance that they enjoy in the German system, for example.

In the *World Competitiveness Report* for 1990, which reflects the opinion of business leaders, Canada scores above the average of industrialized countries in terms of management's freedom "to adjust employment and compensation levels to economic realities." But Canadian employers appear to rely more on external adjustment mechanisms – by laying off workers, for example. This type of adjustment causes disruption in the lives of workers and even in the conduct of business. By contrast, internal adjustment mechanisms – reduced overtime, internal reallocation of workers and tasks, and further training – place less strain on the economy and individual workers, and thus are preferable. When Japanese business leaders praise management flexibility in their country, it is mainly these internal mechanisms that they have in mind. Differences in management freedom thus reflect differences in institutional arrangements.

Canadian labour relations are characterized by adversarial relationships that are not conducive to social harmony. One symptom of this is the large number of days lost to labour strife. This may explain why business leaders perceive that Canadian workers do not identify strongly with the objectives and priorities of their company and why absenteeism is significant – higher than the average for other countries. These factors are additional weaknesses of the Canadian labour market.

## Lessons from Japan and Germany

One may contrast these weaknesses of the Canadian system with achievements in highly successful countries like Japan and Germany: low drop-out rates at both the secondary-school and postsecondary level; strong commitment to science and to research and development; reliance on high-quality vocational training, either as compulsory schooling or under the aegis of employers; highly developed mechanisms of internal mobility based on career advancement; cooperative industrial relations, and so on. All of these characteristics are keys to the strength of the German and Japanese economies. While their respective systems differ markedly, they do have a common characteristic in that success comes through an integrative process in which all of these key features build upon one another in a positive, coherent fashion.

How do these fundamental ingredients build up to global success? In seeking the answer to that question, we concentrate on five main features usually present in both Germany and Japan, although sometimes in different degrees – the role of social cohesion; the diversity of educational paths; the involvement of business in education and training; the importance of the learning continuum in careers; and the role of government.

## Social Cohesion

Social cohesion based on a strong sense of belonging to the community is a key factor bringing coherence to the Japanese learning system. Although not to the same extent nor in quite the same way, German society also clearly signals to its children the goals and rewards attached to education. The involvement of German employers in the provision of vocational education integrated into the compulsory curriculum and the strict organization of the German school system bear witness to this; for example, secondary schools are streamed according to the inclination and abilities of the children, and there is fierce competition for placement in the best training firms.

Japan is well known for its widespread social consensus on the importance of education. This consensus is fundamental in setting the high standards of academic knowledge required from schools. Parents – especially mothers – are deeply committed to enhancing children's prospects through direct involvement in some school activities. Parents are also committed through a significant financial effort over and above their contribution through income taxation: the direct contribution of households to children's education amounts to 1.3 per cent of GNP. This often covers expensive enrolment in private, fee-charging institutions whose popularity also reflects the importance attached to education, as well as attendance at expensive night and "holiday" schools (*yobiko* or *juku*) to supplement the regular curriculum and foster the preparation of Japanese children for selective secondary-school entrance examinations. During their careers, Japanese workers display a keen desire to invest time and money to keep abreast of developments affecting their fields of endeavour.

Canadian society does not show such a widespread, strong commitment to education, and Canadian children do not seem to receive the appropriate signals to perform to the best of their abilities. Among the symptoms of this lack of commitment are the high and enduring drop-out rate from secondary school (around one third, compared with less than 2 per cent in Japan and less than 10 per cent in Germany); weak achievement in international tests in maths and science; and the incidence of illiteracy and innumeracy among the young. High education standards require a social compact in which the whole society shares an understanding of what must be done to achieve a high performance.

## Curriculum Options vs. a Standard System

There is no unique way to get young people ready for the world of work. In that respect, Germany and Japan show quite different patterns leading to a successful transition from school to work – diversity of education options in Germany, commitment to a standard academic curriculum in Japan. But both of these models derive their coherence from the strong involvement of employers in the design and delivery of professional qualifications. For comparison purposes, Figure 13 presents a diagram of the school systems in Ontario, Quebec, Germany, and Japan.

Both the Ontario and the Quebec systems resemble that of Japan in their emphasis on an academically oriented path of study. Why, then, do they not obtain an equally successful outcome? Two factors not found in Canada are crucial in the Japanese case: an explicit sharing of educational and training tasks between the education system and employers; and a strong social commitment to praise and reward school achievement, which makes for high retention rates.

Although at first glance far from the Canadian system, the German model does provide an alternative based on the response to two types of diversity: diversity of students' abilities and interests, and diversity of labour demand in the job market. This model deserves a closer look if Canadians believe that the present problems of transition from school to work are closely related to a curriculum that is

Education and Training in Canada 43

**Figure 13**

**Education systems of Ontario, Quebec, Germany, and Japan**[1]

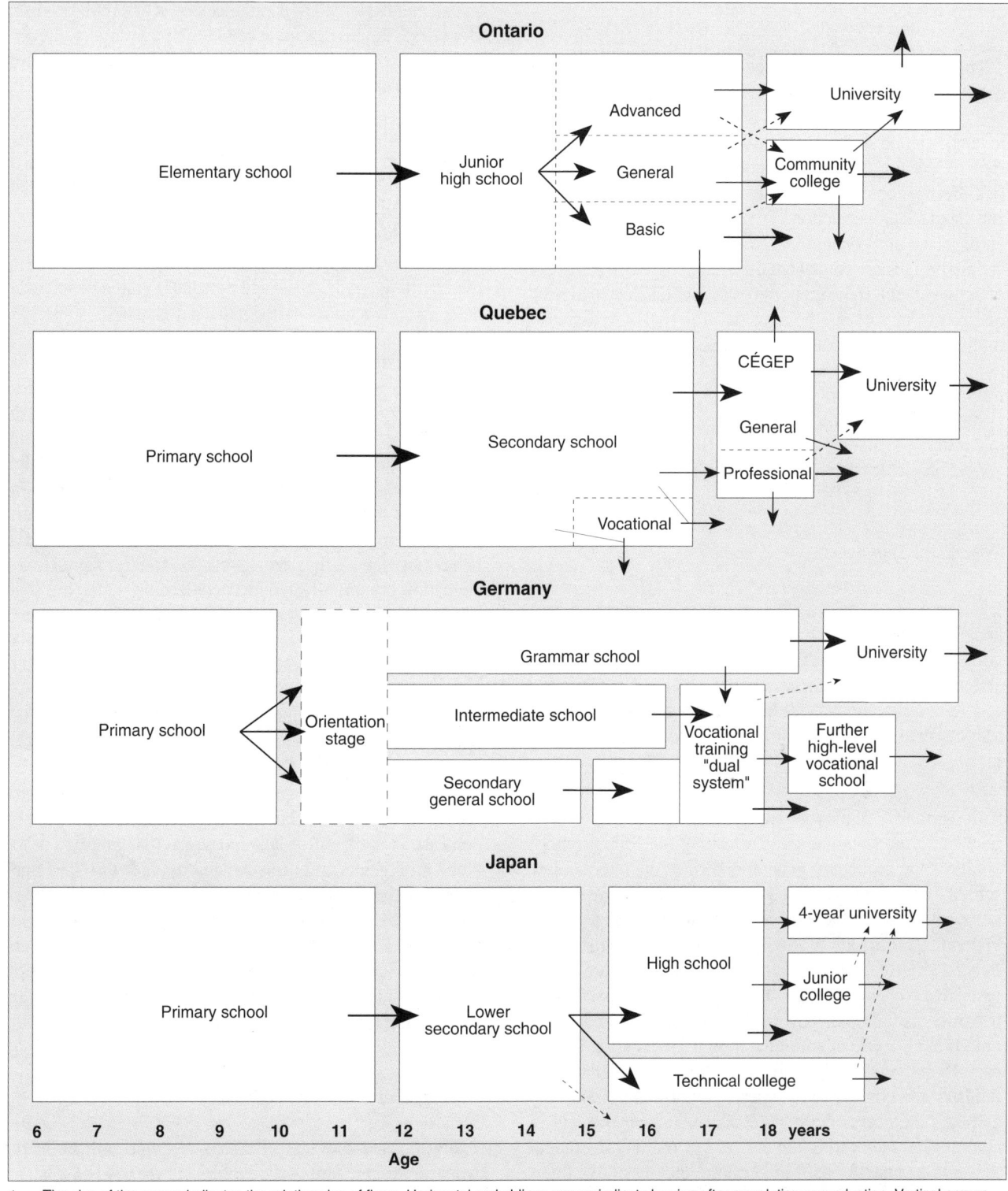

### Ontario

Elementary school → Junior high school → Advanced / General / Basic → University / Community college

### Quebec

Primary school → Secondary school → CÉGEP / General / Professional → University
Vocational

### Germany

Primary school → Orientation stage → Grammar school / Intermediate school / Secondary general school → Vocational training "dual system" → University / Further high-level vocational school

### Japan

Primary school → Lower secondary school → High school / Technical college → 4-year university / Junior college

Age: 6 7 8 9 10 11 12 13 14 15 16 17 18 years

1. The size of the arrows indicates the relative size of flows. Horizontal and oblique arrows indicate leaving after completion or graduation. Vertical arrows indicate leaving before completion or graduation. Arrows not linking two educational levels indicate exit to labour market or inactivity. In Ontario and Quebec, schooling is compulsory until the age of 16; in Germany, full-time until the age of 15, and part-time between the ages of 15 and 18; and in Japan, until the end of the lower secondary school.

too monolithic to meet the requirements of all students, and to a lack of vocational preparation among the large numbers of young people who enter the labour market from secondary school.

The German system proceeds from early streaming between the ages of 10 and 12, based on the children's aptitudes and inclinations. At age 15 or 16, most of those in nonacademic streams enter the "dual system," which consists of learning in the firm under the authority of a certified *Meister*, combined with school attendance for general and theoretical instruction. Two thirds of young Germans enrol in the dual system. Although changes between educational routes are somewhat difficult because of stiff tests of achievement, they are possible at several stages: almost one fourth of students holding the *Abitur* (the "passport" to university admission) become trainees in the dual system; 13 per cent of trainees go on to further education or training after completion of their apprenticeship in the dual system. The obligation made to employers to provide formal training to all employees under 18 extends compulsory education – at least on a part-time basis – until that age.

*Committed Employers*

In the present socio-economic context, in which school and work have become inextricably intertwined, the involvement of employers in the process of learning both general and vocational skills is essential. Once again, Germany and Japan show considerable differences in approach, but a similarly high level of commitment to education and training.

In Germany, employers are committed to provide vocational training to young people leaving the formal school system – the secondary general school or the intermediate school – at the age of 15 or 16. Within a legislative framework set up at the federal level and under the aegis of the Federal Institute for Vocational Training (*Bundesinstitut für Berufsbildung*), the "dual system" is organized through an extensive collaborative effort of social partners involved in tripartite institutions – governments, employers, and labour unions at all levels of administration (federal, state, and local). Employers' organizations, such as the "chambers of industry and commerce" (*Industrie und Handelskammern*) and the "chambers of crafts" (*Handwerkskammern*), play a central role, monitoring the delivery of training in companies and in institutions. Furthermore, they establish training centres to correct any deficiencies and ensure uniform quality standards. These bodies also give accreditation to firms as providers of training in the dual system.

By providing training at their own expense, companies make a substantial contribution to education in Germany; the average cost of training an apprentice is about $13,400 a year, and the length of apprenticeship is two or three years. Of course, the involvement of German employers in training is not confined to the dual system: fewer than one fourth of German companies participate in it. But the deep-rooted commitment to skill development generally is reflected in the fact that, in 1989, the private sector devoted 2.18 per cent of GNP to vocational education and training and to continuing education. This is a reflection of the fact that the business sector is conscious of economic realities and understands its role as a partner in training. This commitment is seen by employers as contributing to social stability by providing employees – and especially young people who have just left school – with status and a place in society.

In Japan, the commitment of employers to education and training takes a quite different form. Companies are not directly involved in the provision of such services before students complete compulsory education or further schooling, either secondary or postsecondary. Employers expect a high standard of academic achievement. Then, they take responsibility for the necessary vocational training after recruitment. By emphasizing educational achievement and social behaviour when hiring, employers send a clear signal to the education community: young people must receive a high level of general education, accept the need for serious work and discipline, and have an appreciation of collective work. In addition, employers establish strong links with schools and postsecondary institutions through recruitment practices. This special emphasis on recruitment reflects the strong commitment of employers to "lifetime employment."

The German and Japanese systems provide key elements for coherence in the school-to-work transition. Canada, by contrast, is in the unenviable position of having one of the worst arrangements for this transition. Since this "passage" is one of the most important steps in life, Canada's poor record in this area is a matter of major concern. Although a wholesale transplantation of any of these systems to our country is impossible, the German and Japanese examples help us to identify some ingredients of success that might serve to improve the Canadian system.

*Careers and Continuous Learning*

About three quarters of Canadians who will be in the work force at the turn of the century are already in the labour market. With rapid changes in the workplace, the capacity to adapt and create high-wage jobs depends more on the skills and aptitudes of these people than on those of future school-leavers. That is why, in response to present and coming challenges, the firm must become a "learning enterprise." Once again, Germany and Japan show us how this concept can be put into practice.

The German dual system is deeply integrated into a learning continuum. Relying heavily on career experience for promotion, companies develop a responsible attitude to training and the acquisition of recognized qualifications. Internal training is complemented by a wide array of vocational training in postsecondary technical schools – often supported by the chambers of industry and commerce – and in universities. A few figures may give an idea of the central place that continuing vocational training occupies in German companies:

– in 1988, 35 per cent of the population aged 19 to 65 participated in continuing-education courses, more than half being directly related with the job;

– two thirds of engineers started their careers through the dual system;

– more than one in four executive managers of the largest companies started as apprentices, and almost half of them went back to study and obtained a postsecondary diploma. One third of these large companies trained their own executive managers.

Several studies have presented evidence that in Germany the occupational training system and the recognition of the human factor in the strategy of the firm encourage the rapid adoption of appropriate technologies and organizational change – keys to improvement in productivity. Moreover, strong and widely recognized qualifications give workers negotiating strength within the firm and a strong position on the external labour market, thus linking high salaries to high qualifications.

The Japanese system shows essentially similar characteristics but places less emphasis on the formal recognition of qualifications and more on seniority for promotion. The firm is an essential focus of the individual's personal and social life. Human resources are a company's most valuable capital and are given the greatest consideration, with training as an indispensable element. Having essentially recruited young people without vocational training, Japanese firms – and not only the large ones – provide extensive training to new recruits. Typically, such training will impart not only technical skills appropriate for work, but also essential elements of the culture and philosophy of the enterprise. The delivery of much of the training internally by managers and supervisors favours a rapid integration of recruits. Thereafter, a succession of planned off- and on-the-job training periods, combined with job rotation, ensure that the abilities of employees are developed on a continuing basis according to the evolving needs of the company.

*The Role of Government*

Japan and Germany show two very different types of administrative organization. Japan is a highly centralized country, where the ministry of education jealously guards its prerogatives – with particularly close control over curriculum and evaluation at the national level. The ministry of labour and local governments are active in the field of occupational training (national testing and certification of qualifications, administration of training centres, financial assistance to small business), but the scope of this effort falls far short of the training activity of the major corporations or groups of corporations.

In contrast, Germany – like Canada a federal state – possesses a decentralized, but coordinated, administrative organization. The primary responsibility in education-related fields rests with the states (*Länder*). The "standing conference of the ministers of education" (*Ständige Konferenz der Kulturesminister*) and a federal presence through the ministry of education and science ensure a high level of coordination. As stated in the "basic law" (*Grundgesetz*), freedom of movement and of occupational choice necessitates co-operation among the *Länder* for the standardization of school and higher education systems in terms of structures, curriculum, and evaluation systems. Also, federal labour legislation regulates, down to fine detail, the working conditions and training of workers, as well as social negotiations at the industry level.

Canada is the only federal country without a federal ministry of education. To make this point is not to argue for another layer of bureaucracy in the field of education, but to emphasize the necessity of coordination to ensure that a pan-Canadian labour market is well served by its education systems everywhere in the country. Coordination mechanisms must be found. Traditionally, provincial governments have tended to be more concerned with their own priorities than with a search for adequate coordination of their respective systems and policies. Recently, however, the Council of Ministers of Education (which does not include a federal representative) has been striving to coordinate some aspects of education policy, such as evaluation and the setting of goals.

In the area of labour market policy, passive employment policies (essentially, unemployment compensation) have predominated in Canada, compared with pro-active policies, such as support for training and employment creation. Both the Japanese and the German cases show the importance of the role of government as an active partner in building coherence between labour-market and education institutions. Although Canada and Germany spend a roughly similar amount on labour-market programs relative to their GDP (2 to 2.5 per cent), Germany spends twice as much as Canada, in relative terms, on active measures – especially training. The Canadian government has been moving towards more active labour-market policies. But the examples of Germany and Japan show that, to be effective, an active stance of the government in the area of training must lean on a strong commitment on the part of employers. The lack of concern of Canadian employers until now may be one reason why changes have been slow, despite the fact that Canada's weaknesses in this area have been well documented for many years.

## Summary

As the first part of this section already suggested, and as the examples of Germany and Japan clearly demonstrated, the positive characteristics of the education system, the labour market, and the economy reinforce one another. This shows the high degree of coherence that is required of the multiple interactions within national socio-economic systems. By comparison, Canada often has a missing link that prevents it from entering the virtuous circle that transforms a wealth of resources into global success.

In fact, Canada (and the United States) on one side, Germany and Japan on the other, may well reflect two quite different models of the transition from school to work, which can be contrasted as in the box. The two North American neighbours rely on the principles of a "market model," while Japan and Germany rely on an "institutional model."

Individual competition in free markets, along with an emphasis on the unconstrained freedom of individual decision making and on local control, is the basis of the market model. A drawback of this excessive emphasis on individualism is that certain people may lack the resources or influence to compete equally in the learning system and the labour market. This weakness can be tempered by the high level of accessibility of the system, which opens up a wide range of opportunities to everyone. However, individuals are largely left alone to confront the world that surrounds them. This is particularly true of students and their parents, faced with crucial orientation decisions regarding curriculum choice, first-job search, and career decisions. Each person proceeds by trial and error. And while Canada has a comprehensive social safety net, financed by taxpayers and managed by governments, that attempts to address problems such as unemployment or poverty, the very existence of this protective net may lull some young people into a state of apathy.

By contrast, the "institutional model," although it does not deny general market rules or individual freedom of choice, is characterized by organized interactions between institutions – firms, schools, unions, or governments. Individuals are still free to make decisions, but they get full support from such a network and clear indications of opportunities and ways to achieve career goals. Rather than being left alone, they develop a strong sense of belonging – to their community, their company, their country – and the sense of responsibility that goes with it.

The key to continuous improvement in the standard of living is a central concern in our evaluation of the performance of the Canadian education system. While there is no "one size fits all" model, the most successful countries offer a few lessons that deserve serious attention, provided the lessons are general in scope, transcending national cultural characteristics. We may summarize a few of these:

– Today's world offers young people a myriad of opportunities for which the education system must prepare them. In Canada, too often young people do not receive clear signals on which to base sound career choices. As a consequence, many get lost in the process of labour-market trial and error.

– With insufficient involvement of employers in the design and delivery of education in the early stages of vocational development, skill mismatches inevitably arise. Moreover, a strong commitment by employers towards continuous learning – largely missing at present in our country – is crucial to fostering the motivation and adaptability of workers.

– The lack of coherence in several aspects of the Canadian education system, and especially in school-to-work transition mechanisms, suggests that governments – together with other stakeholders – must focus on concrete ways to develop closer links between education and the world of work in Canada.

In short, what is needed is a national consensus on the importance of education and training and on the widest possible involvement and commitment in the quest for excellence.

### Models of School-to-Work Transition

|  | Market model | Institutional model |  |
|---|---|---|---|
|  |  |  |  |
| Premises | human-capital theory; individual competition on free markets ↦ better worker/job matching | signal and information networks theories; institutional relations ↦ importance of information and confidence in partners |  |
| Representative countries | Canada, United States | Germany | Japan |
| Type of administrative control | decentralized | decentralized | centralized |
| Formal involvement of educational institutions in the transition process | none | growing, but still limited | strong at all school levels ↦ preliminary employee screening by teachers |
| Formal involvement of employers in the transition process | none | strong, but government employment services important as intermediary | strong and direct ↦ relationships between companies and schools |
| Signals sent by employers to students | vague, no clear criteria or general values; not much consideration for high school grades | clear ↦ direct link between academic results and "quality" of apprenticeship positions | precise and standardized ↦ academic marks accorded high importance |
| Signals received by young people | confused, if any ↦ no incentive/motivation for school work; weak relationship between marks and quality of jobs | clear ↦ strong incentive to work hard; school streaming takes marks into account | clear, teachers used as relay |
| Main means of entry to first job[1] | friends: 27.7% (in the U.S.) family: 15.7% | (not available) | school: 49.2% family: 11.6% |
| Company recruitment policy | according to immediate need | according to need, but considering the social role of hiring young people | regular and annual |
| Layoff practice | fast, based on seniority; young people go first | constrained by legislation and collective agreements; major role for work councils | last resort only; then emphasis on pre-retirement |
| Unemployment rates: young people (15-24)/total population (1990) | United States: 10.7% / 5.4% Canada: 12.8% / 8.1% | Germany: 8.1% / 7.1% (1987) | Japan: 4.3% / 2.1% |

[1] Based on data from Nakajima.

## Conclusions

Many Canadians are not well served by their education system. For example, secondary-school programs are heavily geared to the needs of the 30 per cent of students who will go to college or university. Most of those students will graduate and find interesting jobs and decent incomes. But what about the other 70 per cent of young Canadians.

Our research shows a woeful lack of pragmatic technical and vocational programs to prepare young people for the world of work. Exceptions are few and far between. So it is hardly surprising that about one third of secondary-school students drop out and spend haphazard periods of casual work and joblessness. The failure to provide these students with basic skills means that nearly a quarter of young Canadians are both functionally illiterate and innumerate. *If present trends continue, our schools will release one million more functional illiterates into the work force by the year 2000.* When they do find a job, their employers are unlikely to offer them world-class on-the-job training.

Our findings point to two other weaknesses of the education system. First, the performance of Canadian students on international tests in mathematics and science – essential subjects in the 1990s – is mediocre. These lacklustre academic results, combined with the poverty and paucity of secondary-school vocational programs, gives us the worst of both worlds. Second, the substantial differences in achievement among the provinces suggest serious inequalities in learning opportunities across Canada.

The Council believes that Canadians as a society *and* as individuals must now give an urgent priority to improving the overall performance of their learning system. We propose ways of doing so here. We set out targets for the system, suggest indicators to assess progress towards these targets, and recommend four directions for systematic improvement in elementary and secondary education and in workplace training. The success of these, or indeed of any other, proposals for improvement depends on coherence in education and training.

As suggested at the outset of this Statement, coherence is a coordinated system of communication based on clear signals, effective incentives, and appropriate responses. In practical terms it means, for example, that students (and their parents) receive a consistent set of signals and can easily grasp how to respond to them. This does not happen at the moment. Information about employers' expectations is hard to get and often confusing; students receive little help in their transition to the workplace. High achievement is not always rewarded, and credits are often nontransferable. Some of the most useful courses are underfunded, and those who teach them are often held in low esteem.

To change this situation we need, first of all, a broad consensus among Canadians on the role and value of learning. Next, stakeholders must commit themselves to improving the coherence of the system. Employers in all sectors must articulate their needs and expectations clearly; school boards, counsellors, and teachers must find it to their advantage to interpret and respond to employers' needs; the numerous programs and levels within the education system must fit together so that they offer predictable pathways to students. This entails a wide spectrum of groups working together to diffuse information, design and implement programs, and adjust incentives. Figure 14 shows how complex the interactions between students and other players are.

In a coherent system, these interactions complement each other; in an incoherent one, they confuse and demotivate the student, and often lead to the costly trial-and-error training and job search that is the norm for too many young Canadians.

How can we turn things around? Clearly, the very nature of coherence rules out recourse to a governmental "grand design." The $40-billion learning system is too large – and the needs of Canadians, too diverse – for that. So, neither creating a centralized federal education department nor strengthening the authority of provincial departments would solve the problem. Nor would convening a Canada-wide meeting to draw up educational goals and targets. Rather, Canadians must establish mechanisms to engage the stakeholders – departments of education, teachers, employers from all sectors, unions, parents and students, and social and voluntary agencies – in the pursuit of coherence on an on-going basis.

Such mechanisms have long escaped us in Canada, but there are welcome signs of change. The Council of Ministers of Education is moving towards broad consensus on objectives, indicators, and student testing. The Canadian Labour Force Development Board, which will assess various aspects of the learning system and its links with the labour market, is bringing together a broad spectrum of employers, unions, and educational and social constituencies. And the "learning" component of the federal government's Prosperity Initiative represents an effort to emphasize the national importance of education and training, and to canvass the widest possible cross-section of Canadians. Provincial initiatives – such as the Ontario Training and Adjustment Board and the proposed *Société québécoise pour le développement de la main-d'œuvre*, for example – are a further reflection of a growing understanding of the importance of enhancing our learning potential in a concerted way. A convergence of such initiatives will be an important step towards coherence. Indeed, the emergence of a coherent learning system would represent, in our view, a powerful form of social compact.

In the following pages, we set out some targets, as well as four broad directions for change that would, we believe, improve performance, enhance coherence, and move us closer to these targets.

### Targets

The targets (see box on p. 50) are intended to provide a broad framework for policy making. In some cases – such

**Figure 14**
**Coherence: participants and linkages**

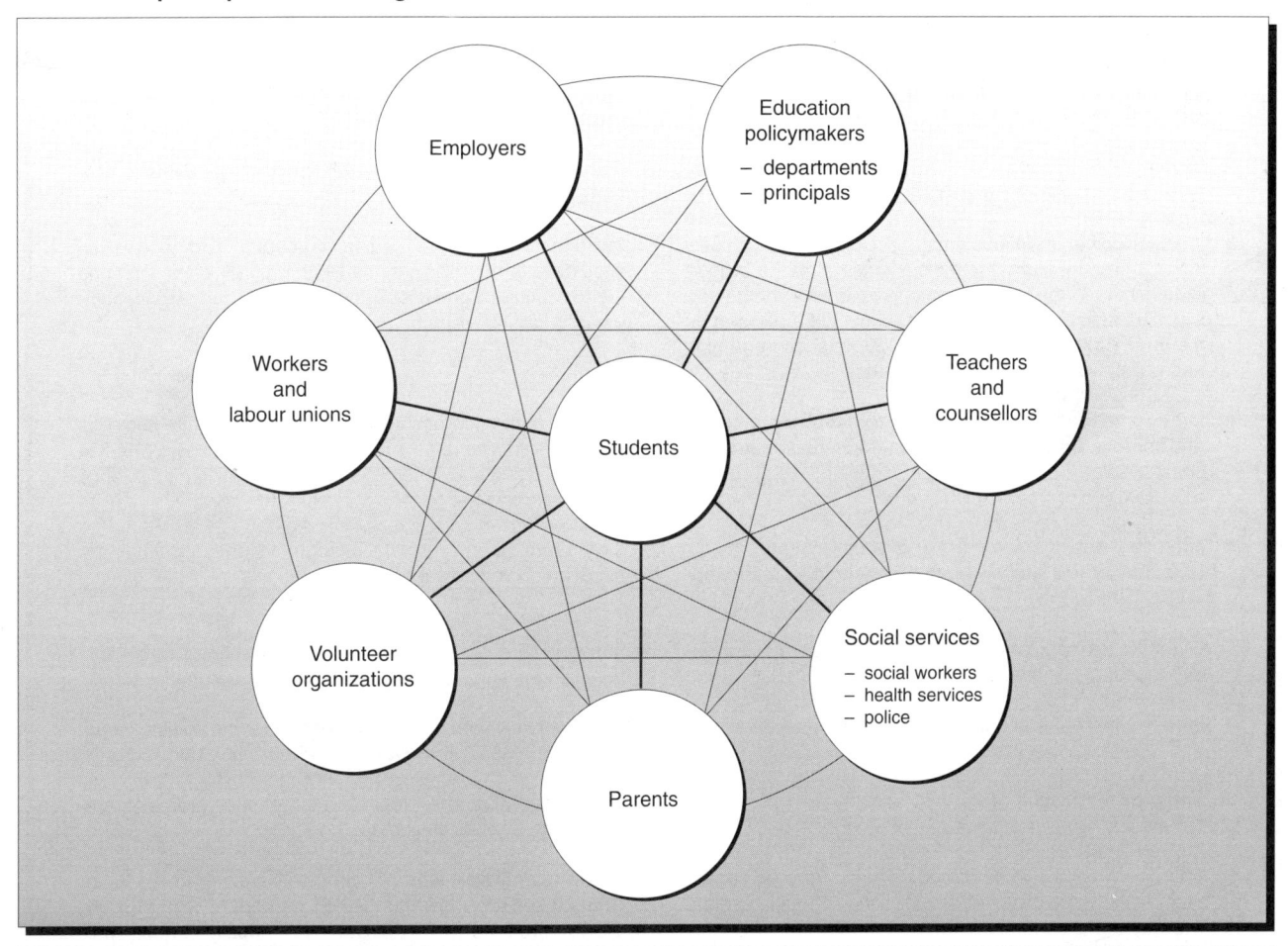

*Diagram showing interconnected circles labeled: Employers, Education policymakers (departments, principals), Workers and labour unions, Teachers and counsellors, Students (center), Volunteer organizations, Social services (social workers, health services, police), Parents.*

as literacy, numeracy, and drop-outs – we propose numerical targets. In other cases, only broad, general objectives can be stated. The list is not exhaustive, but we hope it will set a benchmark for provinces, for school boards, and for individual schools. In some cases, tougher – or simply different – objectives will be appropriate, depending on circumstances and ambitions.

In defining these targets, we have been very mindful that they should be ambitious yet attainable, and we have worked to strike a balance between the two. In our research, we determined where Canada stands currently with respect to a number of indicators of performance of the education system. We then identified targets and goals being set in various jurisdictions – some of these targets are very similar, if not identical, to targets set in some provinces recently – and consulted widely with experts and advisors in the community.

We do not claim that this set of targets is immutable: it is expected that the targets will change through time as progress is made in achieving them. And not all jurisdictions will give equal priority to all targets. In terms of specifics, different provinces and even different regions within provinces face different challenges, and they may well prefer to focus on one problem over another; for example, dropout levels may be very high in one region, while another may find that although drop-out rates are relatively low, achievement levels are unsatisfactory.

We do strongly believe, however, that the set of targets that we have identified serves to outline, accurately and fairly, the core dimensions of the challenges faced by education in Canada in the 1990s. We therefore urge all stakeholders – from schools, parents, and students through school boards and provincial education ministries to employers, unions, and the community at large – to examine

## The Council's Proposed Targets

| Targets | Current status |
|---|---|
| 1  By the year 2000, all 16-year-old Canadians (except for the mentally disabled) should be functionally literate and numerate. | In 1989, some 28.5 per cent of 16 to 24-year olds did not reach Functional Literacy Level 4 and 44.5 per cent did not reach Numeracy Level 3. |
| 2  Increase the proportion of graduates among high-school leavers by 3 per cent per year. | The apparent drop-out rate of high-school students is estimated at 30 per cent. |
| 3  Increase enrolment in mathematics, science, and engineering at university and in technology subjects at the college level; increase the retention rate in advanced maths and sciences at the end of secondary school to 30 per cent by the year 2000 and 40 per cent by 2010; encourage girls and young women to enter these fields. | Full-time college enrolments in engineering and applied science have fallen steadily since 1983; typically, fewer than one fourth of senior high-school students enrol in advanced mathematics and science. |
| 4  Improve achievement, especially of the weaker provinces, and improve Canadian students' performance on international tests. | Literacy, numeracy, and student achievement in mathematics and science show large interprovincial differences; Canadian students' results on international mathematics and science tests are mediocre. |
| 5  Improve the image and content of vocational secondary-school programs and encourage partnerships and cooperative programs. | Only about 10 per cent of Canadian secondary-school students are in vocational programs. |
| 6  Overhaul the apprenticeship system to make it more relevant and responsive. | The coverage of the system is highly concentrated in traditional trades and a few low-skilled service occupations. |
| 7  Improve the quality and quantity of industry-based training. | On a per-employee basis, spending on formal training by private firms in 1987 was less than half that in the United States. |
| 8  Enhance articulation of the education system to simplify transfers among institutions. | Recognition of, and accreditation for, past programs and related experience is piecemeal. |
| 9  Enhance accessibility by raising retention rates and enrolment rates of the disabled, women, and aboriginals to the average of the general population. | Grade 12 retention rates for aboriginals are only about 45 per cent; women are underrepresented in technical fields of study; the disabled are underrepresented in postsecondary programs. |

their own performance in order to see how well it measures up and to assess where their energies should be directed to effect improvements in education performance.

### Indicators

Indicators enable us to monitor progress towards attainment of the targets. A vast array of indicators would be necessary to provide a comprehensive assessment of the education and training systems. The criteria that one invokes to judge performance depend on the objectives of the evaluators: parents, students, teachers, administrators, governments, taxpayers, employers. Each group has expectations of the system that may not always coincide. Moreover, many important outcomes of the system – such as tolerance, civility, fairness, independence, flair, and love of learning – are intangible. We tend to measure what we can, and to report it.

A number of useful indicators can be considered that could be helpful in monitoring progress towards goals. Ideally, one would like to see a highly readable "digest" or "scorecard" of the relevant data on a regular basis (perhaps every five years) so that progress could be assessed. A suggested set of such indicators is shown in the box on p. 51.

Such a set of targets and indicators would, we believe, help school administrators, teachers, parents, employers, students, and policymakers judge the performance of the system and, most importantly, their own performance within it. It could do much to heighten public awareness and,

> **The Council's Proposed Indicators**
>
> *Achievement*
>
> - Literacy and numeracy test results should be published every five years.
> - Drop-out rates should be published regularly; they should be refined to take account of those who "drop back in."
> - Student achievement in basic skills should be assessed regularly for early detection of deficiencies.
> - International, interprovincial, and intraprovincial test results – and results over time – should be assessed in order to permit important comparisons.
>
> *Preparation for the Labour Market*
>
> - Enrolments in secondary-school vocational courses show progress towards a more relevant range of programs.
> - Graduates' occupation by field of study, and placement success, indicate the employment relevance of initial preparation.
> - Type and amount of employer-based training data help gauge the industry's commitment to skill formation.
> - Supplies of highly qualified personnel show how well the education system responds to the skill needs of the information economy.
>
> *Accessibility*
>
> - Female enrolment and graduation in various disciplines indicate women's progress in nontraditional fields.
> - Secondary-school retention rates of aboriginal children and participation rates of the disabled help monitor progress for important minority groups.
> - Socio-economic status of students shows how well the system serves different groups.

thereby, help in the setting of appropriate expectations. Together, heightened awareness, challenging goals, and measures of performance are likely to enhance a crucial ingredient of the system – namely, motivation.

## Directions for Change

Four directions for change will, in our view, result in a system of education and training that is:

*comprehensive* – i.e., addresses the needs of all students;

*open* – i.e., encourages innovation, differentiation, and greater parental involvement;

*responsive* – i.e., adapts to social change and individual needs; and

*relevant* – i.e., recognizes the skill needs of the information age.

## Towards a Comprehensive System

**Canada must move towards a system that provides a closer integration of school, work, and training. The wholehearted commitment and active participation of employers in all sectors – public and private, goods-producing and service-producing – are absolutely essential to the success of such an approach. Employers must continually identify and clearly articulate their needs; communicate their expectations to students, parents, and educators; and commit themselves to active collaboration with educators and with the wider community in the design and delivery of programs.**

In this regard, certain approaches look promising. These include partnerships between employers and the schools (including cooperative education programs) and the integration of a revitalized and expanded system of apprenticeship with secondary-school programs.

*Promote Partnerships* — Partnerships between employers and schools may take a variety of forms – from informal exchanges of information and student visits to the workplace, to highly sophisticated ventures involving jointly planned curricula and credit programs integrating school and work/training experience. Two observations are appropriate in this context. First, such arrangements often depend on the energy and initiative of visionary individuals, so that momentum may be lost when they move on. Thus it is important that school boards come to view such arrangements as a matter of policy; as well, the active involvement of industry and employers' associations and of unions is also needed to provide a context of continuity. (The efforts of the Canadian Chamber of Commerce set a good example in this regard.) A commitment to employer/education partnerships must be institutionalized as one of the essential components of a system in which economic agents and the education system work together in a coherent framework. Partnership is a key ingredient of coherence – one consistent with the Canadian market economy.

Second, partnerships should be defined widely so as to involve not just employers (whether business or nonprofit organizations like hospitals), unions, and the schools, but the wider community of stakeholders, including parents, social agencies, and the voluntary sector. This would enhance awareness and support, promote continuity, and overcome the isolation from the everyday world felt by many teachers and students.

While partnership can take many forms (see box), two – cooperative education and apprenticeship – are particularly important.

*Expand Cooperative Education* — While formal evaluations of cooperative education are few, the evidence to date strongly suggests that all parties benefit. The beneficial effects in terms of reducing absenteeism and drop-out rates may be particularly important. Cooperative programs at the secondary-school level have been developed in Ontario, British Columbia, and Alberta; however, the overall percentage of students involved is very small (less than 10 per cent). Furthermore, with few exceptions, such programs have tended not to focus on the skilled trades. The positive contribution of cooperative education should be encouraged through an expansion in the number of students and in the range of programs. To that end, provincial education authorities should set targets for cooperative programs, giving school boards incentives to seek out the best practice from across Canada and to work with employers and unions to put cooperative education programs in place at the secondary-school level. These efforts should include greater emphasis on exposing students to the skilled trades.

*Link Formal Schooling and Apprenticeship Training* — Fundamental to the creation of greater coherence is the closer integration of secondary-school education and apprenticeship training. Closer links between education and training at the secondary-school level would address two concerns – the academic bias of the secondary-school system and the low status of apprenticeship training.

There is a wide and growing consensus that a fundamental flaw in the Canadian educational system is the excessively academic orientation of the typical secondary-school curriculum. While such an approach is appropriate for the 30 per cent of students who go on to postsecondary studies – though, as we point out elsewhere, we are concerned that even that 30 per cent is not being as well-served as it should be – it fails to serve the needs of the remaining 70 per cent. For the latter, two outcomes are apparent. A disturbingly high proportion drop out of school altogether, whether because of a lack of interest or a lack of ability, or because they are drawn by the prospects of employment. And the remainder who do complete school but do not go on to postsecondary studies find that they have limited job skills. They know little about the labour market and are not equipped to succeed in it.

Our belief that apprenticeship training must be more closely integrated into Canadian secondary schools also arises from concerns about the apprenticeship system itself. Apprenticeship training has a low status in the minds of many Canadians. That reflects faults within the apprenticeship system as well as the fact that most Canadians know little about the types of training apprenticeship offers. As noted earlier, Canadian apprentices are much older than those in other countries. Too often in Canada, people turn to the apprenticeship system only after they realize that they have few skills to offer potential employers. Part of the reason for that, we suspect, is that many students and new entrants to the labour market are simply unaware of what the skilled trades do and what apprenticeship training provides. Earlier exposure to vocational programs, coupled with relevant work experience, would do much to overcome these problems.

Experience to date with apprenticeship programs at the secondary-school level appears to be very positive. In this context, Ontario's Secondary School Workplace Apprenticeship Program, now offered by 25 boards, bears examination. SSWAP students gain credits both towards apprenticeship qualifications and towards secondary-school graduation. We note that almost half of all secondary-school students work part-time; that proportion is higher in the higher grades. Partnerships offer an opportunity to tailor a student's work experience to vocational programs in a systematic way.

Earlier in this document we pondered the question of whether, given global competitive realities, Canada could continue to maintain a learning system markedly different from the most successful models of coherence. While insufficient data have as yet been amassed to permit conclusive evaluations, the apprentice-like alternance of work experience and education that characterizes co-op programs may be a promising move towards a Canadian variant of the dual

---

**Partnerships: A Variety of Forms**

- Career Days: local employers host students
- Providing awards for superior performance
- Summer Science Camps
- Work experience terms for teachers
- Adopt-a-School Programs
- Work-experience terms for cooperative-education students or apprentices
- Secondment of personnel from businesses to schools to teach specialized courses
- Participation of employers and skilled tradespersons in curriculum planning and course design
- Employer visits to schools for guest lectures and demonstrations
- Assisting in the certification of graduates
- Loaning or donating equipment and facilities.

system – one that is consistent with our overall market orientation. This opportunity should not be ignored. Clear and direct links to the regular adult apprenticeship system are of critical importance.

*Broaden the Range of Apprenticeship Training* — The first step towards the closer integration of secondary-school education and apprenticeship training must consist of a broadening of apprenticeship in Canada. Canadian apprenticeship is highly concentrated in a few occupations, primarily in the goods sector. Given the changing nature of the Canadian economy, such a focus is too narrow. Furthermore, the provinces have tended to develop their apprenticeship programs and standards independently, leading to uncertainties about comparability and transferability. Our research reveals that the number of trades granting Red Seals to a majority of their apprentices has been low. The adoption of agreed-upon standards for a skilled trade serves notice to prospective employers that the person certified to that standard has commonly accepted skills, and equally important, can work to recognized safety standards. We do not envision a system involving the imposition of standards upon provinces; but we do see a great deal of scope for wider agreement between provinces on certified apprenticeship standards. Worker mobility within and between provinces would be enhanced, and that in turn could help to shape a labour market that is more flexible in the face of globalization, technological change, and shifts in the industrial structure of employment.

We need a master plan to expand the apprenticeship system, in terms both of the range of occupations covered (including new types of jobs in the service sector) and of standards that are recognized across provincial boundaries. That will require the collaboration of several groups. Currently, certification standards are agreed upon by the Canadian Council of Directors of Apprenticeship, which consists of representatives of each of the ten provinces. But extending the range of certified occupations requires broader input – from the Canadian Labour Force Development Board and its provincial counterparts, the proposed *Société québécoise de développement de la main-d'œuvre*, the professional associations, and the unions.

The creation of closer links with a modernized, expanded, and consistent apprenticeship system is essential for coherence in the school-to-work transition, for students' understanding of the nature of work skills demanded in the labour market, and for their decisions regarding occupational choice and the pursuit of postsecondary studies. A master plan to revamp apprenticeship training in Canada, then, should include the creation of links with secondary-school education. Students should receive credits for any apprenticeship training they complete while in school, and those school programs should be linked to graduates' next stage of training.

*Upgrade the Status of Secondary-School Technical/ Vocational Education* — In many respects, the status of vocational training at the secondary school level has been the victim of a vicious circle. Students considered to be "the best and the brightest" are prepared for postsecondary studies while their academically weaker or more discouraged peers are steered towards vocational programs (when they are available). In a system biased towards academic content and composed largely of teachers with university degrees, vocational teachers, most of whom are the product of apprenticeship programs, are at a disadvantage, irrespective of the quality of their teaching. Shop facilities and equipment often are lacking or outdated – a further reflection of the lower status given vocational training by the educational system and society as a whole. We can no longer afford to shortchange 70 per cent of the secondary-school population. In order to attract more able students, we must improve the status of technical training. Formal linkages to postsecondary apprenticeship training can do much in this respect. Rounding out the preparation of technical teachers to include literacy and numeracy skills where these are weak can also help to improve their status. Partnerships between schools and employers have an important role to play as well by helping students to see that employers regard technical training as useful, relevant, and rewarding.

*Strengthen Career Counselling in the Schools* — Counselling is a critical element in a coherent system, especially given the rapid and complex evolution of Canada's occupational structure and its associated skills, and the need for most individuals to make multiple occupational changes throughout their working lives. Students, adults entering or re-entering the labour force, and those facing a change in occupation, need much better exposure to the range of possibilities in the labour market.

Too often, counsellors in the secondary schools have little formal preparation and many schools give career counselling a very low priority – a reflection of their focus on academic preparation for postsecondary studies. Career counselling must become an integral part of a student's education and a key adjunct to labour-force entry and re-entry. All counsellors should be required to complete a standard core curriculum, to meet provincial standards for certification, and to have regular contact with employers and, if possible, work term assignments. "Career courses" should become a compulsory part of the secondary-school curriculum. Students should receive some exposure to information on career options early in their secondary-school years so that they may be aware of occupational requirements in advance of course selection in later years. At the senior-high-school level, students should be given career counselling to assist them in choosing cooperative programs, apprenticeship training, or academic preparation for postsecondary education.

Special attention should be paid by educators, employers, and governments to those groups whose "learning continuum" traditionally has been interrupted most severely – women, Natives, and the disabled.

*Towards an Open System*

**The educational system will have to change in order to improve its overall performance. Change must involve the recognition of differences among schools and among teachers, as well as the injection of opportunities for students and parents to make free choices. To that end, the local organization (school board, school, etc.) must assume leadership and primary responsibility in education. Education ministries should act to support the local organization and set strategic goals for education within the province.**

The public education system is a large monopoly that is heavily bureaucratized on both the employer and employee sides. The Council believes the system would perform better if it were more open and flexible. It would then be better placed to build upon its strengths and correct its weaknesses. However, we believe the system can be opened up without taking drastic measures to privatize. But it should offer more choice and more scope for differentiation. The measurement of school performance is a critical component of a school system based on choice. We believe the teaching profession could be opened up as well by the explicit recognition of differences among teachers and by professionalizing teaching.

*Introduce School Choice* — In many respects, the education bureaucracy, in its attempt to treat all participants equitably, has ended by treating all equally – regardless of ability, interests, or performance. Thus most students are offered academic courses with few technical/vocational options, and most children attend their neighbourhood school. A more transparent system – one that allowed more *choice* and differentiation – would help to involve parents and students more than does the rather inflexible system that is currently in place. In our view, provincial policy and school-board practice should be designed to increase the opportunity of choice of school for all parents and their children within the public school system. Vancouver and Edmonton are examples of two jurisdictions that have introduced school choice, and their experiences have been very positive. Of course, the opportunities for choice are greater in larger cities than in rural areas and small towns; in the latter cases, differentiation would more often be confined to program offerings within schools, but it could also be improved through distance education.

The advantages of freedom of choice among schools in the public system include increased accountability of principals and teachers for educational outcomes. It would place a high value on excellent teaching. It would help to decentralize responsibility to local schools and to parents. And it would help to identify weak spots in the system so that remedies could be introduced to upgrade schools that are performing poorly; these might include the need for a new principal, for involvement of social agencies to address students' problems, for stepping up remedial classes for students who are falling behind, or for changes in the teaching staff, for example. School choice would also offer the opportunity for, and means of assessing, differences in teaching approaches, in school ethos, and in school organization, and other factors that affect educational outcomes.

Taken further, a system based on school choice would encourage greater differentiation among schools, enabling students to achieve a closer match of their interests and abilities with program offerings. Some schools might attract students who are especially strong in maths and sciences, while others might offer excellence in technical or artistic studies or other important avenues for personal and intellectual development. The important thing is that programs not aiming to prepare students for college or university should be providing clear pathways to future training and employment opportunities. And regardless of their focus, all schools must strive for excellent literacy and numeracy skills.

*Measure School Performance* — Parents and students can choose intelligently only if reliable information is consistently available regarding schools' educational characteristics and achievement. Provincial authorities and school boards should, therefore, provide continuous comparable information on the performance of all fully and partially funded schools in their jurisdictions on the basis of selected relevant educational indicators. Such information must be comparable across schools and through time, and must be made public. The Quebec ministry of education already publishes an array of achievement indicators for the secondary-school level, showing, for example, average student test scores by subject and by school board.

In a system characterized by differentiation of program offerings across schools, it would be necessary to develop a range of indicators that might include, for example, dropout rates, average scores on standardized tests, the percentage of students going on to university, the percentage of students completing the secondary-school stage of apprenticeship training, and the percentage placed in advanced apprenticeship training programs. While such information would be absolutely essential in a system based on school choice, it would also be highly desirable in the current system.

*Professionalize Teaching* — Given the important role played by teachers in Canadian society, we must ensure that the quality of those entering teaching is high. Many factors affect an individual's occupational choice. Among those are the status and pay associated with any given occupation. On average, teachers in Canada are relatively well paid, compared with teachers in other countries and with other occupational groups in Canada. However, they face a fairly flat earnings scale: earnings are relatively high at the lower end of the scale and level off by mid-career. A related concern has been expressed about the appeal of teaching as a profession. The education system is heavily bureaucratized, and little distinction is made between good teachers and poor ones. Too often, the rewards and incentives for outstanding performance are absent; equally, sanctions against poor performance are rarely applied, if at all.

Elementary and secondary teaching is in need of professionalization. Career planning should become an integral part of the relationship between teachers, principals, school boards, and ministries of education. Currently, teachers' careers progress more or less in lock-step fashion, with salary increases being determined according to a standard formula based on years of teaching experience and educational background, including additional qualifications. Means must be found to motivate all teachers to perform to their full potential, to reward superior teachers so that they stay in the classroom, and to urge poor ones to leave it. Career-path planning would facilitate the more careful deployment of the teaching force: superior teachers could, in addition to teaching, act as role models for other teachers and help to train student-teachers; good teachers would, as now, provide the backbone of instruction; and poor teachers would be encouraged to seek opportunities in other fields. Attention to the portability of teachers' pensions will help to ease the transition out of the classroom and into other employment for those for whom teaching is no longer attractive.

Progress towards the greater professionalization of teaching could be achieved through the introduction of categories of teachers, differentiated by performance and ability, education/training, salary, and responsibility. We envision a model based on three levels of teachers: instructors, career teachers, and lead teachers. The *instructor* level would consist largely of beginning teachers undergoing a two-year period of induction, after which, if successful, they would receive full accreditation as teachers. They would combine a smaller teaching load than certified teachers with study, observation, and critical self-appraisal, and would work under the supervision of a senior teacher. *Career teachers* would be those who have successfully completed the requirements for certification and taken on the full responsibility for teaching students. *Lead teachers* would be those who have consistently shown superior performance and ability, motivation, and commitment; they would act as mentors and role models for other teachers in their schools; and they would play an active role in shaping instruction in the school. Teachers do differ in ability; some would move more quickly than others from level to level, and some would never reach the senior ranks. At the same time, incentives and reward systems would be in place to recognize the contributions of the best teachers, giving them a route to advancement that keeps them in teaching rather than, as is now the case, forcing them to seek administrative positions that, while placing them on a new career path, take them out of the classroom where they are most needed.

*Establish Teacher Registries* — The process of matching teacher supply and demand is poorly organized. If an interested and available teacher with the required skills does not happen to see a job vacancy advertised in a given location, then the best hiring decision may not be made. Teachers may leave the profession for either the short or the long term for a variety of reasons, but once no longer employed with a school board, contact with them is often lost. And it is vitally important that teachers be well trained in the fields in which they teach. To match teacher demand and supply more closely and to have consistent information over time regarding teacher supply and demand trends, each province should maintain a "central teacher registry." Such registries would allow the tracking of practising and nonpractising teachers and their records of certification. School boards could register their teacher requirements with the provincial central registry, which could then play an important brokerage role in matching teacher supply and demand.

*Rationalize and Restructure* — Finally, given the funding and cost constraints reported earlier on, efforts to improve the overall performance of the system must be accompanied by redoubled efforts to control costs. School boards and provinces should closely examine the organization of education within their jurisdictions with a view to rationalizing structures and reducing administrative overhead and duplication of services.

The educational system in Canada consists of a multiplicity of school boards divided along linguistic, religious, and geographic lines. At the same time, school boards exhibit differences in cost structures, including the share accounted for by administration costs. We cannot help but believe that, given the size of the educational bureaucracy, a great deal of scope exists for reducing wasteful duplication of services within and across school boards. Throughout Canada, governments and industry alike face the necessity of controlling expenditures, restructuring, and rationalizing their operations. The educational bureaucracy is no different. We urge provinces and school boards to examine closely their own organizational structures in order to identify opportunities to reduce costs. Such opportunities may range from sharing transportation services to amalgamating school boards in some areas.

*Towards a Responsive System*

**In addition to broad directions for change, there is a need to focus on specific targets, notably reducing dropout rates and increasing literacy and numeracy.**

In our assessment of the quality of the learning system, we have observed an array of new and complex factors that pose major problems for educators. Our research into the characteristics of students in major Canadian cities, for example, reveals a wide diversity in their ethnic, cultural, and linguistic backgrounds. Special efforts are required by teachers, parents, and the students themselves to help them realize the potential of the learning environment.

*Be Ready to Learn* — In addition, we have observed the increasing need for teachers to deal with a variety of social problems – drugs, pregnancies, unstable home environments, and child poverty – that were formerly handled by other institutions such as the family and the church. We learned of an alarming need to provide breakfast programs in the schools: too many Canadian children come to school too hungry to learn. For a variety of demographic and socio-economic reasons, therefore, readiness to learn may be a problem at any age. A fully coherent system must place learning firmly in the context of a wider social environment and ensure that the role of the school has the support of other social and community services.

Since learning is a cumulative process, however, we especially emphasize the importance of readiness to learn at a very early age. We therefore urge provincial governments to pay special attention to preschool programs of the Head Start variety.

*Adopt Remedial Measures* — We observe that "dropping out" is not a clear-cut, instantaneous event. Rather, it is a process that begins when a child first "drops behind." All provinces, school boards, and schools should undertake regular *diagnostic assessment* of children's performance in basic skills from the earliest years of schooling. A variety of remedial measures should be developed to prevent students from falling behind. One promising approach is to recognize explicitly that different students progress at different rates, so that some need more time than others to master a particular skill. Rather than giving slower students easier material, they could be given additional time. Other approaches include special tutoring by teachers, teachers' aides, and/or parents; mentoring – which might involve, for example, a more advanced student; supplementary study-groups; and the time-differentiated learning approach described above. This remedial work is the area that should be given the highest priority in allocating new funds and where cutbacks should be avoided.

Recent Statistics Canada surveys of literacy and numeracy have demonstrated that some 3 million Canadians are functionally illiterate and innumerate. If the performance of the school system does not improve and if the drop-out rate does not decline, at least a million new young illiterates will be released into the labour force during the 1990s. *Such an outcome must be avoided at all cost.* Accordingly, provinces and school boards should increase the required credits in compulsory subjects, enrich the opportunity to learn in these subjects, and reduce the number of elective subjects.

*Towards a Relevant System*

**Canadians must commit themselves to continuous upgrading of skills in the workplace, in educational and training institutions, and in the home.**

To succeed in fiercely competitive global markets, Canadians will have to be innovative and flexible enough to exploit new technologies. This means that they must have good foundation skills and that they must continually extend and upgrade their range of specialized skills. In addition, however, it is clear that the new skill requirements place a heavy premium on scientific and technological literacy.

*Improve Performance in Mathematics and Science* — In this context, the school system has an important role to play, both in giving all young people a certain basic level of understanding of how science and technology affect their lives and in fostering an interest in pursuing postsecondary studies in these fields. That is why we have set as an important target the retention of more students in advanced maths and sciences at the senior-high-school level and the attraction of more students to postsecondary studies in those fields.

We note, in particular, the need to encourage more young women to enter the science disciplines.

Of course, the quality of those science and mathematics courses will have a bearing on the level of students' interest in enrolling in them and in working to do well. But many school boards are experiencing difficulties in recruiting sufficient numbers of teachers qualified to teach science, mathematics, and technical courses. Often, the result is that underqualified teachers are asked to teach these subjects or that, especially in the case of technology, the courses simply are not offered. Special measures are needed to address these shortages, which are expected to persist. Faculties of education should focus especially on undergraduate students in science and mathematics when recruiting. In addition, they should set targets for the recruitment of potential teachers in those subject areas where shortages exist so as to better balance supply and demand in each area.

*Increase Workplace Training* — Formal schooling and the inculcation of good foundation skills represent the earlier stages of the learning continuum. Equally important is training for new skills that come with new technology or that enable employees to perform their jobs better. Learning must be regarded as a continuum that extends throughout an individual's lifetime. Workplace training can run the gamut from highly sophisticated in-house programs with resident instructors to informal learning-by-doing. Whatever the form, it should reflect the conviction that the strategic planning of the enterprise must involve the clear identification of skill needs and that success – for individuals, firms, and society – will depend in large part on the continuous upgrading of skills.

Canada's record on workplace training compares unfavourably with that of its major trading partners. Some observers contend that a significant portion of Canada's training effort is not measured by surveys because it is of the informal, "learning by doing" variety, and that it would compare more favourably if this were taken into account. There is little reason to assume, however, that other countries do significantly less than Canada in this regard. The calls for much greater emphasis on development of a *training culture* appear appropriate. But of all the reasons for employer reluctance to invest in human-resource development, the outstanding one is still the issue of what economists call "externalities": the possibility that a firm's investment in people will be captured by a "pirate." This is particularly the case for small firms, which may lose workers to bigger organizations that can offer a broader choice of opportunities for advancement. The federal and provincial governments, in collaboration with the Canadian Labour Force Development Board and its provincial/regional equivalents, should examine ways to create institutional arrangements in order to provide greater incentives for human-resource investments in small firms and to enhance the targeting of training-assistance funds to small firms.

Several models have been proposed to help stimulate more training in industry. One scheme to address the pirating problem is the Employee Training Loan Insurance Scheme; this involves a loan advanced jointly to employer and employee to cover training costs. Repayment is the employer's responsibility so long as the employee does not leave the firm voluntarily. If the employee does leave, then the repayment is the employee's responsibility, with the option to arrange compensation from the new employer. Australia has adopted an alternative arrangement in the form of the Training Guarantee, introduced in 1990. This requires all but very small firms to incur training expenditures equivalent to at least 1.5 per cent of their payroll. Firms that do not meet this minimum target are required to pay the difference to a government fund that will be used to support training. A third model that should be examined closely is Quebec's recent scheme of reimbursable tax credits for training.

Concern about Canadian employers' apparent weak commitment to workplace training is not new. In fact, the Council has raised this issue on a number of occasions in the past, most recently in *Good Jobs, Bad Jobs* (1990) and *Making Technology Work* (1987), where we outlined the benefits of formal training arrangements, such as paid educational leave and training vouchers. We again urge employers to examine their records of commitment to training and to develop employee training programs that will enhance their performance.

*Build on the Potential of Distance Education* — In concluding our comments on the importance of life-long learning and the development of a "learning culture," we draw attention to the potential offered by distance education as a learning tool. This alternative delivery mechanism for the learning continuum is often overlooked by both public and private sectors, although Canada's strength in this area is recognized throughout the world. Further development of distance education might usefully involve the creation of networks of community-based learning centres providing access not only to a range of technologies but also to other learning tools, including libraries, instructional software, and tutorial and counselling services. Information on distance education is sorely lacking, however, and we urge Statistics Canada to include among its educational statistics data on the characteristics of courses, costs, and numbers of students on a regular basis.

## Concluding Comments

During our work, we have frequently been struck by the paucity and poverty of data. While we have enjoyed good cooperation from the provinces in the provision of information, we note considerable variation in the type of data, level of detail, accessibility, and presentation. We have noted the need for better, regular information about distance education, private-sector provision of vocational education and training, training in industry (especially the magnitude of on-the-job training), and vocational education at the secondary-school level. The Council of Ministers of Education should work to create greater harmonization and complementarity in the collection and analysis of data by the provinces.

To obtain more detailed data on the learning continuum, the Council of Ministers of Education, in cooperation with Statistics Canada and a task force of relevant stakeholders, should explore the feasibility of establishing a longitudinal database covering individuals from (say) the age of 5 through completion of "foundation" education and ten years into the labour force. A database comparable to the Swedish Malmö longitudinal study (which now extends over 50 years) would provide a cornucopia of interesting, relevant, and important findings, ranging from the effect of preschool conditions on educational achievement and on labour-market success to the effect of educational methods and reforms, and including information on the effect of education on career development, job satisfaction, and life enrichment.

In this study, we have attempted to assess the ability of Canada's education and training systems to meet the challenges that lie ahead. We have drawn attention to a number of areas where we have found those systems wanting. We repeat the need for commitment and concerted efforts by well-motivated students, well-informed parents, enlightened employers and trade unionists, and dedicated teachers to ensure a solid investment in the future. It is not just a question of paying our taxes and waiting for the system to produce. For sound investment, we must be more demanding, and we must also be active participants. There is no better way, in our view, to secure the present and improve the future prospects of our children. In the words of Confucius: "If you think in terms of a year, plant seed; if in terms of ten years, plant trees; if in terms of a hundred years, teach the people."

# References

Anderson, L. W., and T. N. Postlethwaite, "What IEA studies say about teachers and teaching," in *International Comparisons and Educational Reforms* (q.v.).

Barro, S. M., and L. Suter, *International Comparison of Teachers' Salaries: An Exploratory Study*, National Center for Education Statistics (Washington, D.C.: U.S. Department of Education, 1988).

Canadian Federation of Independent Business, *Skills for the Future: Small Business and Training in Canada* (Toronto, 1989).

Canadian Labour Market and Productivity Centre, "Report of the task forces on the labour market development strategy," Ottawa, 1990.

Crocker, Robert K., "Science achievement in Canadian schools: national and international comparisons," Working Paper no. 7, Economic Council of Canada, Ottawa, 1990.

DesLauriers, Robert C., "The impact of employee illiteracy on Canadian business," Conference Board of Canada, Human Resources Development Centre, Ottawa, August 1990.

Employment and Immigration Canada, Labour Market Policy Analysis, "EIC study on high-school vocational education in Canada," Ottawa, February 1992.

Fullan, M., and F. M. Connelly, *Teacher Education in Ontario: Current Practices and Options for the Future* (Toronto: Ontario Ministry of Colleges and Universities, 1987).

Goodlad, John I., *A Place Called School: Prospects for the Future* (New York: McGraw-Hill, 1984).

Hanushek, Eric A., "The impact of differential expenditures on school performance," *Educational Researcher* 18 (May 1989).

*IEA Classroom Environment Study, The*, L. W. Anderson, D. W. Ryan, and B. J. Shapiro, eds. (London: Pergamon, 1989).

*International Comparisons and Educational Reforms*, Alan C. Purnes, ed. ([Alexandria, Va.]: Association for Supervision and Curriculum Development, 1989).

Kifer, E., "What IEA studies say about curriculum and school organization," in *International Comparisons and Educational Reforms* (q.v.).

Krahn, Harvey, and Graham S. Lowe, "Young workers in the service economy," Working Paper no. 14, Economic Council of Canada, Ottawa, January 1991.

Lapointe, Archie E., Janice M. Askew, and Nancy A. Mead, *Learning Science*, prepared for the National Center of Education Statistics, the U.S. Department of Education, and the National Science Foundation (Washington, D.C., 1992).

Nakajima, Fumiaki, *A Comparative Study on Choice of First-Job and Early Occupational History in Japan, the United States, and Great Britain* (Tokyo: The Japan Institute of Labour, 1990).

Nelson Canada, "Canadian tests of basic skills: Form 5 & Form 7 equating study, 1980-1987," a report to the Economic Council of Canada, 1991.

Ontario Government, *People and Skills in the New Global Economy*, a report by the Premier's Council (Toronto: Queen's Printer for Ontario, 1990).

Organisation for Economic Co-operation and Development, *Education in OECD Countries, 1987-88* (Paris, 1990).

Porter, Michael E., *The Competitive Advantage of Nations* (New York: Free Press, 1990).

Quebec, Ministère de l'Éducation, Direction générale de la recherche et du développement, *Education Indicators for the Elementary and Secondary Levels, 1991* (Québec, 1991).

Rees, R., W. K. Warren, B. J. Coles, and M. J. Peart, "A study of the recruitment of Ontario teachers," Social Program Evaluation Group, Queen's University, Kingston, Ont., March 1989.

Robitaille, David F., and Robert A. Garden, *The IEA Study of Mathematics II: Contexts and Outcomes of School Mathematics*, International Studies in Educational Achievement (London: Pergamon Press, 1989).

Rutter, Michael, "School effects on pupil progress: research findings and policy implications," *Child Development*, v. 54 (1983):1-29.

Sellin, N., and L. Anderson, "The student variable model," in *The IEA Classroom Environment Study*.

Siemens Electric Limited, "Apprenticeship training: Canada vs. Germany," a paper presented at a Labour Canada seminar, Ottawa, 18 June 1991.

Statistics Canada, "Distribution report: Human Resource Training and Development survey," Ottawa, 1990.

United Nations Development Programme, *Human Development Report, 1991* (New York: U.N., 1991).

*World Competitiveness Report, 1990 (The)*, 10th edition, S. Garelli, ed. (Lausanne and Geneva: IMD International and World Economic Forum, 1990).

*World Competitiveness Report, 1991 (The)*, 11th edition, S. Garelli, ed. (Lausanne and Geneva: IMD International and World Economic Forum, 1991).

## List of Tables and Figures

**Tables**

| | | |
|---|---|---|
| 1 | Effects of selected input indicators on education-achievement test results, 187 studies, United States and Canada | 12 |
| 2 | Data on private career colleges, Canada, 1989 | 20 |
| 3 | Apprenticeship statistics, Canada and West Germany, 1987 | 21 |
| 4 | Awareness/usage of Employment and Immigration Canada's "Canadian Jobs Strategy" program among Canadian firms, by size, 1987 | 24 |
| 5 | Age distribution of full-time teachers in elementary and secondary public schools, Canada, 1972-73 and 1989-90 | 26 |
| 6 | Average teacher salaries, selected countries, 1980-84 | 29 |
| 7 | Earnings potential in selected teaching occupations, Canada and provinces, 1986 | 30 |
| 8 | Indicators of public-sector spending on education relative to gross domestic product, selected OECD countries, 1989 | 32 |
| 9 | Total expenditures per student, by school level and by province, Canada, 1989-90 | 34 |
| 10 | Total expenditures per student as a proportion of GDP per capita, by school level and by province, Canada, 1989-90 | 34 |
| 11 | School-board expenditures, by component and by province, Canada, 1986-87 | 35 |
| 12 | Spending per student on administration, Canada, by province, 1986 | 36 |
| 13 | School-board expenditures per student, rural and urban regions in four provinces, Canada, 1987-90 | 37 |
| 14 | Ranking of major OECD countries on three sets of indicators | 40 |

**Figures**

| | | |
|---|---|---|
| 1 | Gross domestic product: distribution by sector, Canada, 1990 | 2 |
| 2 | Employment: distribution by sector, Canada, 1990 | 2 |
| 3 | Education expenditures: distribution by level, Canada, 1989-90 | 2 |
| 4 | School enrolment: distribution by level of study, Canada, 1989-90 | 2 |
| 5 | School and school-leaving probabilities for 100 students entering elementary school, based on findings for 1989-90, Quebec | 5 |
| 6 | Proportion of people with less than Grade 9 education among the "registered" Indian population and the general population, Canada, by province or territory, 1986 | 6 |
| 7 | Science achievement, Canada, by province, 1983-86 | 8 |
| 8 | Results of test of basic skills, in Grade 8 students, Canada, 1966, 1973, 1980, and 1991 | 9 |
| 9 | Correlation between the opportunity to learn and achievement in mathematics among secondary-level students in selected industrialized countries, early 1980s | 15 |
| 10 | The learning continuum | 17 |

| | | |
|---|---|---|
| 11 | Importance of training, by company size, Canada, 1987 | 23 |
| 12 | Total expenditures on education, by school level and by province, Canada, 1989-90 | 33 |
| 13 | Education systems of Ontario, Quebec, Germany, and Japan | 43 |
| 14 | Coherence: participants and linkages | 49 |

This Statement was written for the signature of the Members of the Economic Council of Canada. While their views have had a major influence on the conclusions set out here, they did not have the opportunity to review the final text before the decision to abolish the Council was announced.

## Members of the Economic Council of Canada, as of February 25, 1992

JUDITH MAXWELL, Chairman
CAROLINE PESTIEAU, Deputy Chairman and Director
HARVEY LAZAR, Deputy Chairman and Director

PETER M. BROPHEY
　Public Affairs Consultant
　Director, Xerox Canada Ltd.
　Bond Head, Ontario

LÉON COURVILLE
　Senior Executive Vice-President
　Corporate Affairs
　National Bank of Canada
　Montreal, Quebec

GERMAINE GIBARA
　Montreal, Quebec

RALPH HEDLIN
　President
　Ralph Hedlin Associates Ltd.
　Calgary, Alberta

NANCY R. JACKMAN
　President
　443472 Ontario Limited
　(Investment Corporation)
　Toronto, Ontario

CHESTER A. JOHNSON
　Chairman and Chief Executive Officer
　Western Pulp Inc.
　Vancouver, British Columbia

JUDITH KORBIN
　Associate
　Labour Arbitration & Mediation Services Ltd.
　Vancouver, British Columbia

ADAM LAPOINTE
　President
　Société en commandite de création
　　d'entreprises
　Jonquière, Quebec

L. JACQUES MÉNARD
　Vice-Chairman and Managing Director
　Quebec
　Burns Fry Ltd.
　Montreal, Quebec

MARY MOGFORD
　President
　Mogford Campbell Associates
　Toronto, Ontario

GORDON F. OSBALDESTON, P.C., O.C.
　Senior Fellow
　Richard Ivey School of Business
　　Administration
　University of Western Ontario
　London, Ontario

PIERRE PAQUETTE
　General Secretary
　Confederation of National Trade Unions
　Montreal, Quebec

MARCEL PEPIN
　Montreal, Quebec

ROGER PHILLIPS
　President and Chief Executive Officer
　IPSCO Inc.
　Regina, Saskatchewan

STRUAN ROBERTSON
　Deputy Chairman
　Central Guaranty Trust Company
　Halifax, Nova Scotia

RIX ROGERS
　Chief Executive Officer
　The Institute for the Prevention of
　　Child Abuse
　Toronto, Ontario

DONALD J. SAVOIE
   Clément-Cormier Chair in
     Economic Development
   Moncton University
   Moncton, New Brunswick

KEN W. STICKLAND
   President
   KenAgra Management Services Ltd.
   Edmonton, Alberta

MICHAEL A. SULLIVAN
   Chartered Accountant
   Summerside, Prince Edward Island

H. GRAHAM WILSON
   Burlington, Ontario

KEN WOODS
   International Vice-President, Canadian Office
   International Brotherhood of
     Electrical Workers
   Willowdale, Ontario

# Project Team

### Council Staff

Keith Newton, project director
Patrice de Broucker
Gilles Mcdougall
Kathryn McMullen
Thomas T. Schweitzer
Tom Siedule

Jeannine Bailliu, co-op student
Felix Berezovsky, co-op student
Harry Patrinos, research intern

Dora Morris*, secretary
Lucie Marier, secretary

### Consultants

Bill Ahamad and Miles Wisenthal, Ahamad Consultants Inc.
Barbara Brunhuber, University of Ottawa
Robert Crocker, Memorial University
Jane Gaskell, University of British Columbia
Bertha Joseph, Aboriginal Management Consultants
Nelson Canada
Graham Lowe and Harvey Krahn, University of Alberta
David Robitaille, University of British Columbia
Tim Sale, Tim Sale and Associates
Robert Sweet, Lakehead University
François Vaillancourt, Université de Montréal

*Retired before the project was completed.

Special thanks are also due to the staff of the Council's Informatics, Publications, and Public Affairs Divisions.